בס"ד

Early
Chassidic
Personalities

A GLIMPSE INTO
THE LIFE OF
REB PINCHAS REIZES

compiled
Sholom DovB

EARLY CHASSIDIC PERSONALITIES
A GLIMPSE INTO THE LIFE OF REB PINCHAS REIZES

Published and Copyrighted © by
Rabbi Sholom D. Avtzon
450 Sterling Street
Brooklyn, N.Y. 11225
(718) 953-6663

1st Printing 5758 • 1998
2nd Printing 5766 • 2006

Cover Design: Spotlight Design
Illustrations: Mordechai Friedman

Printed in Canada

TABLE OF CONTENTS

INTRODUCTION

The Alter Rebbe, Rabbi Shneur Zalman, once lamented to his son Rabbi Dov Ber (who became his successor and is known as the "Mitteler Rebbe"), that *his* Rebbe, the Maggid, had cultivated sixty great disciples. However, the Alter Rebbe concluded, he had not succeeded to that extent. To this declaration, his son responded, "You also have!" And Rabbi Dov Ber began mentioning them by name.[1]

Who are all of these sixty disciples? We do not know with certainty. In *Beis Rebbe*, the author, Reb C.M. Hilman, lists fifty-five exalted chassidim of the Alter Rebbe. It is not known if all those listed were amongst the sixty chassidim mentioned by the Mitteler Rebbe. However, one thing is sure: all sixty were great giants and to be equally respected.

Yet, when it came time to decide whose complete[2] biographical sketch would be the first one in this series of "Early Chassidic Personalities," the choice was obvious: Reb Pinchas Schick.

---

1. *Likkutei Sippurim,* p. 51.
2. Unlike Reb Shmuel Munkis, the inaugural personality in this series, whose biography is extremely sketchy.

Reb Pinchas is best known to chassidim by the name "Reb Pinchas Reizes." He was a towering scholar in all areas of Torah — *Nigleh* and *Chassidus*. He was a phenomenal philanthropist who readily gave vasts amount of money to charity as well as giving generously of his time and energy to help other Jews. The time he devoted to spreading the teachings of the Alter Rebbe is also remarkable.

But all of these accomplishments do not demonstrate his true uniqueness, as other disciples of the Alter Rebbe also excelled in these areas. His greatness is that he preserved hundreds if not thousands of the Alter Rebbe's teachings and sayings. In addition he is the source of numerous stories and accounts connected to the growth of Chassidism during those essential, formative years. Perhaps, for this reason, the Mitteler Rebbe bestowed on him the title of "The General of chassidim."

Notwithstanding all of this greatness, Reb Pinchas personified the two character traits which the Alter Rebbe demanded from all his chassidim: honesty and humility. This can be seen from the following story:

Once, the Alter Rebbe appointed Reb Pinchas to serve as his personal attendant on important journeys concerning the welfare of many Jewish communities.

On one such journey, the Alter Rebbe noticed Reb Pinchas eating a piece of pastry. "In my *halachic* work,[3] I brought down the different opinions concerning whether the blessing of *Mezonos* or *HaMotzi* is required on certain doughs. Since this difference of opinion exists, I concluded that a person should not eat any pastry besides a honey mix without first washing for bread. Why don't you follow that ruling?" inquired the Alter Rebbe.

"As I recall," Reb Pinchas answered, "the Rebbe writes that a *baal nefesh* [literally, a master of the soul, i.e., a person who is more stringent than required by *Halachah*] should act in this manner. Knowing my own shortcomings, I don't consider myself in that category."[4]

The Alter Rebbe turned to Reb Pinchas and, with a penetrating look, said: "Had I not considered you such a person, I would never have requested you to serve as my personal attendant."

One may ask, why did Reb Pinchas not wash anyway, especially as he was in the presence of the Alter Rebbe? The answer is that his humility and honesty did not allow him to act otherwise. Because of his humility, Reb Pinchas did not consider himself on the level of a *baal nefesh* and due to his

---

3. *Seder Bircas Hanehenin*, ch. two, laws seven-nine.
4. *Reshimos Devorim*, HoRav Chitrik.

honesty, he would not behave contrary to how he perceived himself.

We find a similar situation concerning whether or not one is to put on Rabbeinu Tam's *tefillin*. There also the Alter Rebbe writes[5] that a *yirei shomayim* — a G-d-fearing person — should don them. Since one cannot give himself this title, it was customary for a person to wait to don them until he was instructed by the Rebbe.[6] However, this changed on Purim תשל"ו-1976, when the Rebbe said during the *farbrengen*, "Everyone should begin to don Rabbeinu Tam's *tefillin* as soon as possible," i.e., upon becoming *Bar Mitzvah*.[7]

Following the format which we established in our well-received book on Reb Shmuel Munkis — the inaugural personality in this series — we have divided this book into two parts: the first part contains stories about Reb Pinchas and the second part contains his biography.

A book on Reb Pinchas would not be complete if it didn't include the famous and inspiring story of

---

5. *Shulchan Aruch*, 34:4.
6. The Rebbe would respond to the individual's inquiry, "Should I begin putting on Rabbeinu Tam's *tefillin?*" In most cases, the *Mashpiim* would advise the student to ask this question when he turned eighteen. In *Eretz Yisroel*, some *Mashpiim* had their student ask at fifteen-sixteen.
7. It is now the prevalent custom to begin donning Rabbeinu Tam's *tefillin* at the same time one begins to don Rashi's *tefillin*, two months before the *Bar Mitzvah*.

Emunas Tzaddikim — Faith in *Tzaddikim* — concerning how Reb Pinchas and other chassidim faithfully carried out the Alter Rebbe's instruction.

I take this opportunity to thank *Sichos in English* for allowing me to reprint the story in its entirety from their translation of *Likkutei Dibburim,* Vol. II, as it appeared there. Not only does it give us a clearer picture of who Reb Pinchas was, it vividly illustrates the love and devotion the Rebbeim have for every chossid and also what it means to be a real chossid.

The picture on the cover is of a chossid who is *davening* because, as you will soon read, Reb Pinchas was an exceptional *"davener,"* or in Chassidic terms, an *"oved."*

Reb Pinchas was not blessed with children. Although he requested blessings for children from the Alter Rebbe and the Mitteler Rebbe, his requests were never fulfilled. (The Alter Rebbe mentioned that Reb Pinchas' *neshamah* was from the supernal world of women and therefore he and his wife could not have children. The Alter Rebbe then comforted him by quoting the prophet Elkanah's saying to his wife Chana, "You are more beloved to me than [one who has] ten children."[8] *Likkutei Sippurim HoRav Perlow.*)[9]

While he did not have any physical children, in a sense we are all his children, as our Sages say that whoever teaches his friend's child, it is as if he gave birth to him.

Indeed, Reb Pinchas taught us much, but most importantly we can learn from him how a chossid is to live and conduct his life.

In keeping with the requests of many readers of our first volume, I noted the sources of the stories. The biography was adapted from *Sefer HaToldos* of the Alter Rebbe.

I invite our readers to bring to my attention any stories not included here about Reb Pinchas which they know of to be included in a future printing.

I thank my dear friend, Reb Mordechai Friedman, for illustrating some of the stories in this book. However, we must note that they are for the enjoyment of the reader only. They can not realistically depict how the people in the stories looked, as we have no portraits of them. Yet, his drawings bring the stories to life.

---

8. *Shmuel I* 1:8.
9. HoRav Perlow also writes that on a different occasion when Reb Pinchas lamented about not having any children, the Alter Rebbe promised him עמי במחיצתי — you will be with me even in the World to Come.

As mentioned earlier, Reb Pinchas preserved a myriad of teachings of the Alter Rebbe. Perhaps one of the most important ones for us today concerns the teaching of our Sages that we are day workers.

The Alter Rebbe explained it as follows: "Our duty is to bring daylight into the world."

By fulfilling the Alter Rebbe's directive of bringing the light of Torah and Chassidus into the world, we will succeed in fulfilling the mission with which the Rebbe entrusted us: bringing the revelation of Moshiach *Tzidkeinu* speedily in our days.

Rabbi Sholom D. Avtzon

Yud-Tes Kislev 5758 (תשנ״ח-1997)
Entering the bicentennial celebration
of the Alter Rebbe's release from prison

INTRODUCTION TO SECOND PRINTING

The enthusiastic response to the idea of a young reader's version of the biographies of Chabad's earliest chassidim was evidenced by how quickly the first printing of *Reb Pinchas Reizes* sold out. This, and the success of the inaugural volume on Reb Shmuel Munkis, encouraged me to expand the concept into the series known as EARLY CHASSIDIC PERSONALITIES, soon adding the title of Reb Meir Raphaels to the collection. Volumes on Reb Hillel Paritcher, Reb Binyomin Kletzker and others are in various stages of production for future publication.

In this second edition of *Reb Pinchas Reizes*, stories have been added and many details have been clarified, giving us a fuller picture of who he was and how rich was his connection to both the Alter Rebbe and the Mitteler Rebbe. Typographical and other errors have also been corrected. I thank all those who brought them to my attention.

In the merit of our efforts to emulate the ways of the great chassidim of Chabad, may we hasten the coming of *Moshiach Tzidkeinu*.

Rabbi Sholom D. Avtzon

Chai Elul, 5766
308 years since the birth of
the Baal Shem Tov and
261 years since the birth
of the Alter Rebbe

A Hidden Tzaddik Is Revealed

Once, the Alter Rebbe chose his close disciple, Reb Pinchas, for the very important mission of collecting money for the needy of *Eretz Yisroel*[1] and making sure it was delivered there.

Reb Pinchas was honored to accept the mission. He did, however, ask the Alter Rebbe for a personal "favor." "I will be traveling through the area where the *Tzaddik* Reb Leib Sarah's lives. As I have heard that he conceals his identity, I would like to know how I can recognize him."

The Alter Rebbe replied, "I cannot guarantee that you will meet Reb Leib Sarah's. But I will tell you how you will be able to identify him if your paths cross. He is very tall, has a loud voice, and is often helping the poor. If you meet a man who fits this description, it is probably Reb Leib Sarah's."

---

1. After the *Tzaddik* Reb Menachem Mendel Harodoker and many other chassidim moved there in 5537-1777, the Alter Rebbe took upon himself the responsibility of helping them financially.

The Alter Rebbe blessed Reb Pinchas with success on his vital mission and then told him to stop by the Rebbetzin. Rebbetzin Sterna gave Reb Pinchas food[2] which she personally prepared and would stay edible during his long journey.

Reb Pinchas traveled to all the cities, towns and villages which the Alter Rebbe had instructed him to visit and collected money there. Now he could fulfill the second part of his mission: getting the money to *Eretz Yisroel*.

Although the actual collecting of the money had been crowned with success, one thing bothered Reb Pinchas. He still had not met Reb Leib Sarah's. He was confident, however, that the Alter Rebbe had not given him the description of the *Tzaddik* for nothing. Surely he would meet the *Tzaddik* at some point on his journey.

At every inn along the way, Reb Pinchas inquired if anyone knew of the *Tzaddik* Reb Leib Sarah's or of anyone who fit his description. But the answer Reb Pinchas always received was "no."

One evening, his journey brought him to yet another inn. It was very crowded and there was only one large room still available. Reb Pinchas rented it and requested that he not be disturbed for the next few hours as he would be learning. The

---

2. I was told it was baked cottage cheese wrapped in a dough crust.

extra expense of the large, private room was of no consequence to him as he was by his own means an extremely wealthy man.

After a few hours had passed, Reb Pinchas approached the innkeeper to inquire, as he always did, about the *Tzaddik* Reb Leib Sarah's. This time, to Reb Pinchas' delight, the innkeeper said, "Yes, I know someone who fits that description. His name is Leibel. However," he continued in astonishment, "we do not consider him a *Tzaddik*. In fact, we call him 'Leibke, the Wild One.'"

Reb Pinchas returned to his room with hopeful anticipation. The *Tzaddik* Reb Leib Sarah's comes to the area, if all goes well he would have the *zechus* of meeting him.

In the middle of the night, as he was finishing his learning, Reb Pinchas heard a loud commotion outside. Looking out the window, he saw a group of around forty people. A tall man with a boisterous voice was saying, "Friends, if you're hungry or tired come into this inn and I'll get you some food and a place to rest."

After making sure that everyone had something to eat and a place to sleep, the loud fellow approached the innkeeper and asked if there was an extra bed for himself.

"Leibke," the innkeeper replied, "all the rooms are rented out. But one of the rooms does have an extra bed. Since you're such a good customer, I'll ask the gentleman who rented the room if he would mind if you stayed with him."

Reb Pinchas had heard the entire conversation from his room. The innkeeper only had to knock once before an excited Reb Pinchas opened the door. "Excuse us," apologized the innkeeper, "but do you remember the Leibke I told you about? Well, he is here and would like a bed. So I...."

Reb Pinchas had wondered if the man he had seen from his window was the *Tzaddik* Reb Leib Sarah's. Now he was thrilled to have the opportunity to be in his company. Even before the innkeeper could finish his sentence, Reb Pinchas answered excitedly, "Of course, by all means. Let him come in."

Reb Leib Sarah's entered the room. He matched the description that was given by the Alter Rebbe. Reb Pinchas was now almost certain that his guest was indeed the great *Tzaddik*, but he was hesitant to ask him his name.

Instead, he began, "I see that you have just come from a journey. Though you only asked for a bed, perhaps you would like something to eat?" Pointing to a box amidst his luggage, Reb Pinchas continued,

"Over there is a box of different kinds of food. Please help yourself."

"If you don't mind, I'll take this."

Reb Leib Sarah's thanked him and went over to the box. He carefully rearranged the contents, putting some to the side and removing other items. He seemed to be looking for something specific. Reb Pinchas watched, intrigued, until he saw his guest holding the remnants of the food that the Rebbetzin had prepared for him. The *Tzaddik* then said, "If you don't mind, I'll take this."

Now Reb Pinchas was convinced beyond a shadow of a doubt of the identity of his guest. For who other than a *Tzaddik* would be able to sense which food had been prepared by the Rebbetzin? Reb Pinchas said, "Do I have the honor of meeting the *Tzaddik* Reb Leib Sarah's?"

With a look of astonishment, Reb Leib Sarah's said, "What would make you think that?"

Reb Pinchas explained, "Before I began this journey, which was undertaken at the request of my Rebbe, the *Baal HaTanya*, I asked him to give me a description of the *Tzaddik* Reb Leib Sarah's. You fit that description. Then, when from all the food I have, you specifically chose only the food that the Rebbetzin prepared, I was convinced that you are the *Tzaddik*."

Reb Leib Sarah's replied, "Since the *Tzaddik*, the *Baal HaTanya*, gave you these clues, I will not deny that I am [Reb] Leib Sarah's. Now would you please tell me what mission you are on?"

"The Rebbe entrusted me with collecting the *tzedakah* that chassidim generously give for the needy in *Eretz Yisroel*," explained Reb Pinchas. "*Boruch Hashem*, I collected a sizable sum. Now," concluded Reb Pinchas, "I have to make sure it is delivered."

Reb Leib Sarah's suggested, "Why don't you give me the money and I will take care of it?"

"Since you, who are a *Tzaddik*, are requesting this of me, I will do it," agreed Reb Pinchas. "However, I must give the Rebbe an accounting of the money."

"Don't worry," said Reb Leib Sarah's. "I will give you a receipt stating that I received the money from you." He then wrote on a piece of paper that he had received the *tzedakah* money and took the six hundred gold coins.

Reb Pinchas was now satisfied with every aspect of his mission. He began his journey back to Liozna and the Alter Rebbe.

When, upon his arrival, he entered the Alter Rebbe's room, the Alter Rebbe inquired about the trip. Reb Pinchas happily replied that he had been extremely successful in every respect. He then gave the Rebbe a detailed accounting of how much money was given and by whom.

Finally, Reb Pinchas added, "I would like to thank the Rebbe for enabling me to meet the *Tzaddik* Reb Leib Sarah's." Saying that, he handed the Alter Rebbe the receipt and told him the whole story.

After looking at the receipt, the Alter Rebbe said, "While the *Tzaddik* Reb Leib Sarah's is definitely going to use the money to help the needy, he did not write that he is going to send it to *Eretz Yisroel*. Now, since it was given by chassidim specifically for the poor of *Eretz Yisroel*, you had no right to give it away, even for other extremely worthy causes."

Reb Pinchas responded, "Since the Rebbe feels that I was wrong to give it to him, I will replace the six hundred coins with six hundred of my own."

Later, when he brought the money to the Alter Rebbe, the Rebbe gave Reb Leib Sarah's receipt to him and said, "This is yours." Reb Pinchas treasured that receipt, for he knew that fulfilling the wishes of Reb Leib Sarah's could bring him no loss. Somehow the *Tzaddik* would repay him.

From my father, Rav Meir Avtzon ע"יה

BE PREPARED

Once, when Reb Pinchas was walking with the Alter Rebbe, a poor person approached him and asked for *tzedakah*. Reb Pinchas apologized saying, "I'm sorry, but at this moment, I don't have any money with me."

The Alter Rebbe told Reb Pinchas, "It is not proper for a person like you to walk outside without any money. As you see right now," the Alter Rebbe continued, "had you had money with you, you certainly would have generously helped him. Because of your negligence, that poor man received nothing and is still in dire need."

Reb Pinchas took the Rebbe's admonishment to heart. From that time on, he was always sure to carry money with him.

Likkutei Sippurim, HoRav Perlow

I Need the Mansion, But Not for Me

Reb Pinchas used some of his fabulous wealth to build a brick mansion for himself. As most of the other houses in the city of Shklov were made of wood, his home stood out. In truth, in Shklov any mansion was a sign of affluence, but a brick mansion was something really spectacular.

When he mentioned to the Alter Rebbe his plans to build the mansion, the Rebbe asked him, "Pinchas, why do you need a brick mansion?"

"Rebbe, believe me," explained Reb Pinchas, "when I thought about building my house, I shed more tears than there will be bricks. I keep reminding myself, 'Do I need a brick mansion?'[12]

"But because I will have a mansion, important community meetings will take place in 'Pinchas' mansion.' Since the meeting is taking place in 'Pinchas' mansion,' Pinchas has a say. Once Pinchas has a say, the Chassidishe *melamed* has a job!

---

12. The reasons not to have such a house are discussed later on in the story, "Humble Youself."

"Now, if Pinchas doesn't have a mansion, the meeting won't be taking place in Pinchas' home. Then Pinchas won't have a say and the chassidishe *melamed* won't necessarily have a job."

The Alter Rebbe responded, "You are right; it is a proper thing for you."[13]

Likkutei Sippurim

---

13. There is a *Maamar* in *Likkutei Torah, Devarim* p. 98d starting with the words *Mizmor Shir Chanukas Habayis.* The Rebbe notes that this *Maamar* is also found in the transcriptions of Reb Pinchas with a heading, "Said at the dedication of a brick mansion, on the twentieth of Teves תקס״ז" (1807). It is believed that this *Maamar* was said at the dedication of Reb Pinchas' house.

All the Way

Reb Pinchas once made a calculation of his entire personal fortune, (excluding his house, which belonged to his wife). His wealth totaled ten thousand rubles, which was an extremely large sum at that time.

He then took the total amount and brought it to the Alter Rebbe saying, "Rebbe, I am putting my entire fortune at your disposal. Please take it and do with it as you see fit."

The Alter Rebbe replied, "No, it shall remain with you. You should be blessed with much success and continue doing your good deeds with it."[14]

The Alter Rebbe's words were fulfilled. Reb Pinchas was successful and continued to help others with an open hand to the extent that after he passed away, chassidim saw his personal ledger and the total amount of *tzedakah* that he gave away was almost ten times the ten thousand rubles.

Shmuos V'Sippurim

---

14. See footnote #39.

**The Alter Rebbe replied,
"No, it shall remain with you."**

THE ART
OF GIVING

The Alter Rebbe instructed Reb Pinchas to go to Dubrovna and visit the chossid Reb Zalman Welkis. There he would learn how to properly give *tzedakah*.

When he came to Reb Zalman, Reb Pinchas saw that he had three boxes. Each box contained a different denomination of coins: copper, silver or gold.

Depending on the needs of the person who had come to him for *tzedakah*, Reb Zalman went to one of the three boxes and took out a generous handful. Without looking or counting, he gave it to the person and wished him success.

Reb Pinchas also began dispensing *tzedakah* in this manner. "However," he related, "I have not attained the greatness of Reb Zalman, for after I pick up the money, I still glance to see how much I am giving."[15]

Beis Rebbe

---

15. According to another version (*Likkutei Sippurim*), Reb Pinchas did not glance at the coins. However, at the end of the day or week he counted how much remained in each box.

   In *Shmuos V'Sippurim,* Vol. I, p. 257, it is noted that the other chossid was his brother-in-law Reb Binyomin Kletzker and not Reb Zalman.

BEING
CONNECTED

The Alter Rebbe put limits on how often a chossid could come to him and how long he could stay on each of these visits.[16] However, for those who were extremely close to the Alter Rebbe, such as Reb Pinchas, these restrictions did not apply.

In addition to being with the Alter Rebbe for all three *Yomim Tovim*, Reb Pinchas remained there for the entire month in which the *Yom Tov* took place and for the month of Elul as well.

One year Reb Pinchas was not feeling well, and could not travel to the Rebbe for Elul. Then to his great distress, due to an early and bitter winter, he could not go for Tishrei either.

On *Shemini Atzeres*, while he was sitting in the sukkah and eating the *Yom Tov* meal, Reb Pinchas suddenly cried out, "Oy Rebbe!" To everyone's amazement, Reb Pinchas told them, "The Rebbe is thinking of me right now."

---

16. This is known as *takonos* Liozna.

Indeed, at that very moment, the Alter Rebbe was also in his sukkah *farbrenging*. Suddenly he said, "Pinchas Reizes needs a physical healing. What I am unable to give him, I don't give. However a *brocha* for physical health I can give him."

Amongst those who were present with the Alter Rebbe were chassidim from Shklov. They were very intrigued that the Alter Rebbe mentioned Reb Pinchas in middle of the meal.

After the *Yom Tov* ended, the chassidim all began their journeys home. On their way, they stopped at Reb Pinchas' house, and asked him to honor them with a *l'chaim*.

To the delight of Reb Pinchas and the other chassidim who had been unable to be with the Rebbe, they repeated some of the teachings they had heard from the Rebbe during *Yom Tov*. During the friendly conversation that followed, they mentioned that the Rebbe had spoken about Reb Pinchas at a *farbrengen* on *Shemini Atzeres*.

To their astonishment, some of the chassidim who had remained in Shklov remarked, "We know, since at that moment Reb Pinchas cried out, 'Oy, Rebbe!'"

As it was customary amongst chassidim in those days to help a fellow chossid rid himself of any trace of pride or ego, they began to chide Reb Pinchas, saying, "Is it befitting for you to boast that you know the Rebbe was thinking about you?"

Reb Pinchas answered, "It is not 'I' [who felt it]. You see," he proceeded to explain to his fellow chassidim, "when I had my first *yechidus* with the Rebbe, I entrusted to him with my *nefesh*. At my second *yechidus*, I gave him my *ruach* and at my third *yechidus*, I surrendered my *neshamah*.

"Since I gave my three levels[17] of *nefesh*, *ruach* and *neshamah* to the Rebbe, it is not 'I' who knows."

When telling this story, the Frierdiker Rebbe concluded by saying that this is what is called an "inner feeling."

Sefer HaSichos, 5705, pp. 54-55

---

17. A *neshamah* of a person is divided into five parts: *nefesh, ruach, neshamah, chaya, yechidah*. The lower three are able to constrain themselves inside the human body. Therefore it is possible for the body to conceal the G-dliness in them.

    The two higher levels cannot be constrained by the body. They are the source and cause of a person's sudden inspiration to come closer to Hashem.

A Lesson
in
Humility

Reb Pinchas' father, Reb Chanoch Henoch Schick, was a strong opponent of the Chassidic Movement.[18] Even after Reb Pinchas became a chossid, his opposition remained steadfast.

Reb Henoch once asked his son, "What do you see in *Chassidus* that is so special? You claim that *Chassidus* teaches a person how to serve Hashem, but surely you can learn how to serve Hashem by studying the holy *sefer, Reishis Chochmah*, which is not a Chassidic work!"

Reb Pinchas suggested to his father that he study any topic in *Reishis Chochmah* for two weeks. Reb Henoch chose the topic of humility saying, "You will see that even humility — a trait that chassidim

---

18. We should note that although he was strongly opposed to the Chassidic Movement, he refused to sign or have anything to do with any of the bans that the *misnagdim* gave out against chassidim.

In addition, when his son became a chossid, he *paskened* that *halachically* one is not to sit *shiva* because of it. (This was contrary to the custom of many *misnagdim* of that time.)

pride themselves in — can be thoroughly acquired from a non-Chassidic source."

Reb Pinchas felt very uncomfortable at these words. His father was a great *gaon*. Here he was suggesting that his son test his humility. How else could Reb Pinchas perform such a test if not by putting his father in a humiliating situation? When the two weeks had drawn to a close, Reb Pinchas reluctantly summoned a wagon driver who occasionally took his father on short trips. He told the driver that on their next trip, he should drive wildly, so that the journey would be as uncomfortable as possible. The wagon driver was bewildered by this strange and disrespectful request. We have no idea what must have gone through his mind. But since Reb Pinchas was the Rav's very beloved and learned son, he concluded that there must be a good reason behind it all.

His opportunity to fulfill the request came soon enough, on a hot sunny day. Instead of bringing the comfortable coach with padded seats, the wagon driver arrived in an open wagon loaded with hay. Not wanting to embarrass the wagon driver, Reb Henoch mounted the wagon silently.

As soon as Reb Henoch was seated, the driver began to whip the horse into a fast gallop. The wagon sped through the streets, with hay flying in all directions. Small pieces stuck in Reb Henoch's beard and clothing. As the hot sun beat down upon him, Reb Henoch held on for dear life, fearing that he too might soon fly out of the wagon.

When they finally arrived back at home, Reb Henoch swallowed his feelings and graciously thanked the driver, just as he always did.

Reb Pinchas, who had seen everything, went over to his father to ask *mechila* [forgiveness]: "Forgive me dear father," he said. "It was I who arranged this whole thing. I asked the driver to do this, since you had hinted that I should test you concerning humility. I deeply apologize for any discomfort."[19]

His father looked at Reb Pinchas with astonishment.

The younger man continued, "It is true, father, that you accepted the way he treated you most graciously, and you even thanked him despite everything. But tell me, father, how did you really feel?" Reb Pinchas asked with a disarming smile.

Reb Henoch replied, "Yes, I held myself back from rebuking the driver. But he really deserved to get it. As Bilaam said to his donkey, 'If I only had a sword in my hand...!'"

---

19. According to a different version, Reb Pinchas tested his father by requesting a strong person to jovially "slap" his father on the back.

"How did you really feel?"

Reb Pinchas replied, "You see, father, now you can understand the accomplishment of *Chassidus*. A person who learns *Chassidus* wouldn't find anything here to be insulted, upset or angry about. He would accept the whole thing from Heaven with a heartfelt smile."

Hearing these words, Reb Pinchas' father readily forgave him and no longer questioned the accomplishments of *Chassidus*.[20]

Reshimos Masios

Ironically, it once happened that Reb Pinchas himself was put to this test — by none other than his close friend, the noted chossid, Reb Shmuel Munkis.

---

20. In *Beis Rebbe*, it is written that in the final years of his life, Reb Chanoch wanted to meet the Alter Rebbe. However, due to his frail health at that time, he wasn't able to make the journey.

Humble
Yourself

Once, Reb Shmuel traveled to Shklov and
decided to stay with his close friend, the noted
chossid Reb Pinchas Reizes. Although Reb Pinchas
was not at home when he arrived, the household
servants welcomed Reb Shmuel and invited him to
make himself comfortable.

Reb Pinchas was a very wealthy man and had
one of the largest and fanciest homes in Shklov.[21]

Reb Shmuel wondered, why would a chossid
want to live in such an ostentatious manner? Was it
to enhance the honor of chassidim? In that case,
there might be some merit in it. But money is a very
great test. If you get used to it and enjoy it, it can
have very negative effects on your spiritual level.

Reb Shmuel decided to find out where things
stood.

Since the servants had told him to make himself
comfortable, he went to one of the bedrooms and

---

21. See pp. 10-11, for an explanation of why Reb Pinchas built a
brick mansion.

lay down, deliberately not removing his dusty shoes, which of course dirtied the bedspread.

Reb Pinchas' wife happened to pass by the bedroom. When she saw that their visitor had fallen asleep without removing his shoes, she was aghast.

As soon as her husband returned, she complained bitterly that their guest had soiled the beautiful and expensive bedspread.

Reb Pinchas went to the room and saw that it was none other than his dear friend, Reb Shmuel Munkis. He did not disturb Reb Shmuel, but left him to sleep comfortably.

His wife's words made an impression, however, and when Reb Shmuel woke up, Reb Pinchas chided him mildly, "You must have been very tired, my dear friend, for you fell asleep without even taking off your boots... uh... the bedspread... uh ... became a little... soiled...."

Reb Shmuel was shocked. What had happened to his friend? Were these his priorities?

"After everything the Rebbe taught you, and all the time he spent guiding you, is this what you learned? To worry about your linen!?!"

Reb Shmuel's words found their mark as Reb Pinchas stood there in silent shock. "You ought to have asked me the news of what I saw or heard by the Rebbe. My dear friend, how did you fall so low that the first thing you need to discuss with me is your fancy bedspread?

"I refuse to stay in this house a minute longer. You can keep your money and your pride. I see clearly that you don't want me here, and this was only an excuse to tell me to leave."

**Reb Pinchas humbled himself and
paraded through the streets of Shklov.**

Reb Shmuel got up and began to walk out. "Please don't leave," begged Reb Pinchas. He knew at once that Reb Shmuel was right. "How can I make amends?" he asked.

"If you really mean it," Reb Shmuel answered, "take a broomstick, place it between your legs like a child playing 'horsy,' and parade that way through the streets of Shklov."

For any grown man, that would be a great humiliation. For Reb Pinchas, how much more so. He was not merely "well-off," he was one of the richest men in town and was renowned for his good deeds. In addition, he was a great *Talmudic* scholar, the son of Reb Henoch, the Head of the *Beis Din* of Shklov.

Nevertheless, when Reb Shmuel Munkis chastised him, he did exactly as ordered, humbling himself in public, in true Chassidic spirit, in order to correct a flaw in his character.

From chassidim

A CHOSSID OBEYS

Reb Pinchas had been married for many years and was not blessed with children. The great chossid and Rov Reb Hillel Paritcher suggested to Reb Pinchas that perhaps he should follow the advice of our Sages of divorcing his wife and marrying another woman.

A chossid does not do anything important, especially something of such magnitude, without first asking the Rebbe's advice and blessings.

Reb Pinchas went to the Mitteler Rebbe and told him of Reb Hillel's suggestion. The Mitteler Rebbe did not agree to the recommendation and instructed Reb Pinchas not to divorce his pious wife.

Around that time the Mitteler Rebbe remarked to some chassidim that the intensity of Reb Pinchas' *davening* gave birth to a tremendous number of *baalei teshuvah*.

Sefer HaSichos 5703, p. 125

Inspiration

In the city of Lubavitch lived a wagon driver by the name of Nochum Nochumavitch. One ordinary weekday, Nochum entered the *shul* when Reb Pinchas was in the middle of *davening*. He became so inspired by Reb Pinchas' *davening* that he also had a strong urge to pour out his heart to Hashem.

The simple wagon driver took a *siddur* and turned to the *Mussaf* service of *Yom Kippur*. He recited the *Avodah* with great concentration. He cried emotionally when he recited *Al Cheit*. He fell to the floor for *Korim*. Even though he was an unlearned person, at this moment he reached a very high level of *davening*.

When Nochum the wagon driver finished *davening*, he declared that he could no longer be on the same level as his horse. He could not remain on the simple, ordinary level of the past.[22] He gave up his job as a wagon driver and found a position as the caretaker of a *shul*.

---

22. As you will read later in "Faith in Tzaddikim," sections 35-36, Reb Pinchas also had a life-changing experience. That happened after he merited to be present at the Alter Rebbe's *Hakkofos*.

The Frierdiker Rebbe concluded this story by quoting the Mitteler Rebbe: "Even a great *Talmudic* genius would envy the level this simple Jew attained."

Sefer HaSichos, 5703, p. 125

Please Stop Disturbing Me

Chassidim say[23] that many people made a point of being extra careful when *davening* near Reb Pinchas. For if a person who was *davening* in Reb Pinchas' proximity had a stray thought, Reb Pinchas would turn to him and say, "Oy! Please stop, you are disturbing me."

Peninei HaKesser

---

23. The previous story illustrated the saying of our Sages: "Words spoken from the heart, enter — penetrate and affect — the heart of the listener."

From this story we see that just by being in his proximity one was elevated.

THE DIFFERENCE IS IN ONE'S DAVENING

Reb Hillel Paritcher once commented on the greatness of the *davening* of his fellow chassidim. Through listening to Reb Binyomin Kletzker's[24] *davening*, he explained, one's mind was broadened. However, Reb Binyomin's *davening* could only affect the intellectually elite.

Reb Pinchas' *davening* was something else altogether. It uplifted everyone, even the simplest person, for it opened the hearts of all who heard it.

Sefer HaSichos, 5703, p. 127

---

24. Reb Binyomin was known for his intellectual abilities. He would concentrate on a teaching of the Alter Rebbe for many hours.

   Reb Binyomin is one of the chassidim whose life story will בעזה"י be published in this series of *Early Chassidic Personalities*.

You're Lucky It Was You

After the *histalkus* of the Maggid of Mezritch, his disciples decided that each one of them should continue teaching *Chassidus* in their own respective cities and surrounding areas. Understandably, there would be some differences between them as one of them would place more emphasis on one aspect of the Maggid's teachings, while another one would highlight a different point.

As the years passed, some of these differences became more and more apparent and created some friction. One of the main disputes between them concerned to what extent *Chassidus* should be taught.

Many of the Maggid's disciples followed the examples of the Baal Shem Tov and the Maggid who taught *Chassidus* to only a select group of highly gifted students. The majority of the chassidim of these Rebbes received their inspiration through their faith in the *Tzaddik*. This approach is that of *Chassidus Chagas*.

The Alter Rebbe's philosophy was to explain *Chassidus* in a way that could be understood by all. The Alter Rebbe pointed out that he began disseminating *Chassidus* in this manner at the Maggid's request during the Maggid's lifetime. This is the approach of *Chassidus Chabad,* that of striving to elevate oneself through the study of *Chassidus* rather than relying on *emunah* in the Rebbe for inspiration.

While many of his colleagues agreed that the Alter Rebbe should continue to teach *Chassidus* in his unique way, some of them disagreed. HoRav Boruch Mezhibuzh, a grandson of the Baal Shem Tov, was one of the most outspoken in his opposition to the philosophy of *Chassidus Chabad*.

Once, after the Alter Rebbe had been released from his imprisonment, he met HoRav Boruch. HoRav Boruch told the Alter Rebbe that although he was extremely happy that the Alter Rebbe had been vindicated and released, he was, nonetheless, critical of the Alter Rebbe's approach, especially as the Alter Rebbe began explaining *Chassidus* in even greater detail after his release.

The Alter Rebbe replied, "Your holy grandfather, the Baal Shem Tov, visited me while I was imprisoned and instructed me to do so, telling me that I am to spread his *Chassidus* throughout the world."

Reb Pinchas, who was accompanying the Alter Rebbe and knew the differences of opinion between the Alter Rebbe and HoRav Boruch, noticed that the exchange between them was becoming very strained. Reb Pinchas was fearful that HoRav Boruch might utter harsh words against the Alter Rebbe as other disciples of the Maggid had when the Alter Rebbe refused to join them in proclaiming a counter-ban against the *misnagdim*. Reb Pinchas therefore stepped in between the two *Tzaddikim*.

The Alter Rebbe rebuked Reb Pinchas and said, "How did you have the brazenness[25] to stand between HoRav Boruch and myself? If it had been someone other than you who is so dear and precious to me, I would have chastised you."

Migdal Oz

---

25. In *Shmuos V'Sippurim*, Vol. 1, it is mentioned that one of the Alter Rebbe's chassidim wanted to speak on the Alter Rebbe's behalf and defend his position. The Alter Rebbe, however, did not allow him to do so.

    He later explained: "You are mistaken in thinking that our differences are only a simple disagreement. This is the same controversy that was between Shaul *Hamelech* and Dovid *Hamelech*."

SAYINGS

Reb Pinchas' scholarship and deep understanding of Torah earned him the respect of even the greatest opponents of *Chassidus*.

Reb Pinchas once said that on the opinions of all the *Acharonim* (*Talmudic* scholars of the previous 150 years) there are strong questions which may discredit their opinions. On the commentaries of the great sage the *Shagas Aryeh*, there is place for only a few disagreements.

On the Torah thoughts of the Alter Rebbe, however, there are no valid questions, even insofar as the slightest alteration of his opinions, and there is so much to learn from the choice of his words.[26]

Heard from chassidim

---

26. The Rebbe would refer to the Alter Rebbe's wording in the *Shulchan Aruch* as "his golden expression."

Indeed, *Rabbonim* throughout the years learned various *halachos* from the wording in the *Shulchan Aruch*.

THE GREATNESS OF REB PINCHAS

The *gaon* Reb Chanoch Henoch recognized his son Reb Pinchas' outstanding intellectual abilities at a tender age. In addition to hiring the best teachers for him, Reb Henoch also had a set time every day to personally teach and instruct him. At the young age of twenty, Reb Pinchas was chosen to be the representative of the city of Shklov at the important meetings of the *Vaad Haarutzos*.[27]

His greatness was so extraordinary that the recognized *gaon* Reb Yosef Kolbo,[28] who was many years his senior and originally his tutor, took him as a learning partner.

* * *

The Frierdiker Rebbe expressed the greatness of Reb Pinchas by mentioning the following episode: "When the Alter Rebbe was requested by the

---

27. This was the Jewish Council for many communities. It was authorized by the government to enact laws and directives for their communities.
28. More about him later on.

Rabbonim of Vitebsk in 5569 (תקס"ט-1809) to settle the difference between them and the lay leaders of the city, the Alter Rebbe chose to come with three other people [to assist him].

"They were his brother, Reb Moshe; his grandson, the [Rebbe the] Tzemach Tzedek; and his exceptional student, Reb Pinchas."

* * *

In a letter[29] dated Thursday of *Parshas Lech Lecha*, 5567 (תקס"ז-1806), the Alter Rebbe informed Reb Pinchas that on the previous night he saw in a clear vision [(not a dream)] his teacher the Maggid together with his son, Reb Avrohom the Malach. The Alter Rebbe stood facing them. The letter reads: "My master and teacher told me: 'For the sake of peace you should not change your place of residence and move to the city of Shklov.' My master and teacher continued, 'The reason for this is that your student Reb Pinchas would accomplish there everything that you would.'" Concluding the letter, the Alter Rebbe thanked Hashem for blessing him with such a disciple as Reb Pinchas.

More aspects of his greatness are mentioned in the chapter "A Faithful Student."

---

29. Printed in *HaTomim*, p. 780. This letter is part of the *Cherson Geniza*.

THE FIRST
ENCOUNTER[30]

The city of Shklov was one of the most distinguished cities in Jewish Lithuania. It boasted a great number of brilliant scholars who were respected even in distant lands.

One of the most acclaimed study halls in Shklov was the *Perushim shul* where most of the great scholars learned. These scholars were divided into two groups: the "late sitters" who learned every night until midnight and the "early risers" who arrived at three in the morning to begin their study.

One blustery winter Tuesday night in the month of Cheshvan, תקל"א-1770, a young visitor entered the *shul*. A scholarly and hospitable individual by the name of Reb Yeruchem Dov, a fisherman by trade, immediately went up to him saying, *"Sholom Aleichem."*

Seeing that the visitor was a learned young man, Reb Yeruchem Dov asked if perhaps he could solve a

---

30. The next few chapters are taken from *Sefer HaToldos* of the Alter Rebbe. They were translated in greater detail in the Biography of the Alter Rebbe.

difficulty he had on a certain *Talmudic* saying in the tractate of *Erchin*.

At the mere mention of the topic in question, the visitor immediately began to recite from memory the entire passage of the *Talmud* with Rashi's commentary, translating every phrase. Listening to the visitor's translation of Rashi, Reb Yeruchem Ber realized that his "profound" question was not really a question at all. It was based on a misunderstanding of the entire concept.

Dumbfounded, Reb Yeruchem Ber swiftly approached the revered scholars with whom he had discussed this question and who had been unable to find a satisfactory answer. He related how the young visitor had translated the passage and Rashi's commentary in such a clear and concise manner that his question ceased to exist.

At once, all the scholars gathered around the young visitor to ask their own questions. They listened attentively as he answered them and explained many *Talmudic* concepts. They were astounded by his brilliance and clarity.

Even the genius Reb Yosef "Kolbo"[31] praised the visitor's approach, saying it was superior to the way they were accustomed to learning.

When Reb Pinchas, who belonged to the "early risers," came to *shul*, he was shocked to see that all of

---

31. His colleagues called him this as it means he is knowledgeable in all aspects of the Torah.

the "late sitters" were still there. They were sitting around a table listening intently to a visitor. As the visitor was just beginning to explain a new topic, Reb Pinchas decided to forego his regular lesson and listen.

He was so enthralled by the guest's three-hour explanation of the topic under discussion that immediately after *Shacharis*, Reb Pinchas went to tell his father what had taken place in *shul* the previous night. Reb Pinchas reviewed for his father, HoRav Chanoch Henoch, the *Av Beis Din* of Shklov, the visitor's explanation and novel approach. HoRav Henoch was exceptionally pleased with these explanations and invited the young visitor to have a learned discussion with the scholars of the city. Nobody, however, knew who the young but exceptional scholar was. All he would say was that he was a student and not a *Rov*.

The following day, on Thursday morning, the scholars prevailed upon the visitor to deliver the daily lesson. For five hours he taught the *Mishnah*, *Gemara* and the commentaries of the *Rishonim* on that topic. Though it was an extremely lengthy lecture, it was presented in such a clear way that there was no difficulty in following it.

Late that afternoon, the young visitor left town. It was only some time later that the scholars of Shklov discovered his identity. It had been the *ilui* (genius) of Liozna (as the Alter Rebbe was then known). He was then only 26 years old and a disciple of the Maggid of Mezritch.

Years later, after he himself became a chossid, Reb Pinchas described how this incident once again aroused bitter opposition against *Chassidus*. The *misnagdim* felt they had been intentionally outwitted and they were livid with frustration. How could they have accorded a young chossid so much honor and praise, which in turn gave respectability to the entire Chassidic movement, when they were vehemently opposed to it? They suffered another tremendous setback when it became known that the great genius and sage, Rav Yosef Kolbo, spoke on his behalf. Although at that time he himself was not ready to become a chossid,[32] Rav Yosef reminded the *misnagdim* that their negative opinion of *Chassidus* could not refute the fact that their young visitor was a genius of the highest caliber.

Reb Pinchas remained in the opposition camp as did the majority of the city. However, the seed had been planted and nine years later, he, too,[33] became a chossid. How this happened will be discussed in the next two chapters.[34]

---

32. He became a chossid twelve years later.
33. In Rabbi C.M. Hilman's *(Beis Rebbe)* list of the Alter Rebbe's Chassidim, many of them are from the city of Shklov.
34. See *Likkutei Dibburim*, English edition, vol. II, pp. 150-160, for all the details of this encounter.

THE SECOND ENCOUNTER

In the years that followed, major events occurred relating to the growth of *Chassidus* and the opposition of the *misnagdim*. After the *histalkus* of the Maggid in 5533-1772, his disciples decided that each one should continue to teach and spread *Chassidus* in his own city and its environs.

HoRav Menachem Mendel Horodoker was the leader of *Chassidus* in Lithuania, and the Alter Rebbe was given the position of coordinator. Four years later, in 5537-1777, due to the intensity of the opposition, Reb Menachem Mendel moved to *Eretz Yisroel* and the Alter Rebbe became the leader of the chassidim in Lithuania.

In those early years, the Alter Rebbe delivered extremely short discourses. One of these discourses seemingly provided his opponents with the opportunity they were waiting for. The *Mishna*[35] states: "[On Shabbos] all animals bearing a collar may go out wearing it or may be led along by it." The Alter Rebbe explained that on the level of

---

35. *Shabbos*, chapter 5, mishna 1.

remez, this law can also be interpreted as relating to the songs of angels. With this in mind, he gave the following interpretation: "All the masters of song go out in song and are drawn in song. This is referring to angels in Heaven. They may be elevated or drawn down into this world through song."

When one of his disciples publicized this discourse, it caused an uproar. The *misnagdim* used this interpretation to bolster their claim that the chassidim were trying to change the interpretation of the holy Torah.

Shortly afterwards, the Alter Rebbe himself passed through Shklov. Although most of the scholars there opposed his Chassidic teachings and were especially infuriated by his explanation of the above-mentioned *Mishna*, they respected his greatness in Torah. Therefore, they came to him with all of their difficult *Talmudic* and *Halachic* questions. But to their great surprise and dismay, this time he did not try to respond to even one of them!

Not wanting to miss an opportunity to hear the Alter Rebbe's brilliant explanations, they decided to invite him to give a lecture in a large study hall. They also requested that after the lecture he reply to the questions they had just asked. The Rebbe accepted the invitation and promised to answer all their questions.

Word quickly spread throughout the city that although the *Liozna Maggid* (as the Alter Rebbe was then called) had not answered even one question, he would be giving a public lecture and he would then respond to all inquiries.

The study hall was packed. Virtually all the scholars were present, waiting to hear the brilliant lecture and to see if the Alter Rebbe could answer all their questions in one discourse. Of course, they would also take him to task for his "unorthodox" explanation of the laws of collars of animals.

The Alter Rebbe arrived at the study hall, went up to the *bimah* and said, "Do you want me to give a lecture to answer all your questions? [No,] instead, I will sing a *niggun*, as the *Mishna* states, 'even angels are elevated through song.' "

He began singing an awesome *d'veikus niggun*. Utter silence reigned as all the scholars sat, enthralled by the melody. A sweet stillness entered the hearts of all who heard the *niggun*. Momentarily they forgot where they were and each one was transported into his own innermost thoughts.

Not knowing how, they soon realized the *niggun* had elevated and broadened their intellectual capacities and understanding. By the time the Rebbe concluded his *niggun*, everyone's questions were answered and all their difficulties were resolved!

Years later, when Rav Yosef Kolbo was already a devoted chossid, he related to the Alter Rebbe's second son-in-law the chossid Reb Avrohom Shainis of Shklov, "I came that day with four extremely difficult questions which I had been toiling on for months. I had presented these questions to the leading scholars of Vilna and Slutzk, but to no avail. Yet, when the Rebbe sang his *d'veikus niggun,* all my questions were resolved.

"At that time I felt as small as a young child. That *Mattan Torah niggun* of the Rebbe helped me resolve to become a chossid of the Rebbe," concluded Rav Yosef Kolbo.

While most of the other scholars were not ready to join Rav Yosef and become chassidim, their respect for the Alter Rebbe grew immensely. No longer would they question his Chassidic interpretations. For Reb Pinchas, and many others who had been at that "lecture," all they needed to become chassidim was one more encounter with the Alter Rebbe.

BECOMING
A CHOSSID

As *Chassidus* became more and more widespread, the *misnagdim* intensified their opposition. They publicly urged and encouraged people to engage in activities which would put an end to the growth of Chassidism.

Chassidim suffered greatly from this opposition. The Alter Rebbe and the other disciples of the Maggid met in 5543 (תקמ״ג-1783) to discuss what to do. At that time it was decided that the Alter Rebbe should try to prove unequivocally the falseness of the slander being propagated against *Chassidus*.

The Alter Rebbe instructed twenty of his most gifted students to traverse the countryside in the manner of traveling preachers. After delivering inspiring lectures on self-improvement and how to better serve Hashem, they were to mention that since serious accusations were being made against chassidim, the Chassidic leaders should be called to a public debate. Then, once and for all, everyone would see the faults of *Chassidus*, since "their" leaders were certainly no match for the great scholars and sages of the *misnagdim*.

The people, having heard for many years how ignorant chassidim were, agreed to this proposal. It was decided that the debate would take place that summer in the city of Minsk. Hoping to humiliate the Alter Rebbe, the *misnagdim* chose three elderly, respected sages to debate him. Of course, they had no clue that the whole idea for this debate was the Alter Rebbe's.

The terms they set for the debate were as follows: The Alter Rebbe would have to answer their Talmudic questions to prove that he was worthy to debate with them; then he would be called upon to defend the innovations of Chassidism.

The Alter Rebbe agreed to these conditions, but stipulated that after he would answer their *Talmudic* questions, he would be able to pose to them his own *Talmudic* questions as well.

The debate took place in a large *Beis Hamidrash* which was filled to capacity. Many scholars attended, even some from distant cities who had heard of the Alter Rebbe's greatness. They desired to discover the truth for themselves.

The three sages were well-prepared. They had many difficult questions on diverse topics which they had discussed with numerous scholars but had nevertheless been unable to resolve. They were certain that as great as the young Maggid of Liozna was, he would also be unable to answer some of them. It would be a decisive victory.

To their shock and dismay, the Alter Rebbe immediately answered all their questions with such clarity and ease that all present were able to understand the answers. The sages were amazed not only at his brilliance and vast knowledge, but also at how uncomplicated he made everything.

After answering their questions for five hours, the Alter Rebbe presented three questions of his own to them. The three scholars were unable to respond and said they would present their answers on the following day.

The next day, the *Beis Hamidrash* was overflowing. Everyone wanted to hear how the sages would answer these three very difficult questions, as all the scholars had tried their best but to no avail. The three sages had reviewed the questions the entire night and early morning, but they too had not come up with answers.

At this time, the *Beis Din* of Minsk declared that they were satisfied that the Alter Rebbe was indeed a sage. Now they would proceed to the second part of the debate and he would have to defend the innovations of Chassidism. The answers to the three questions, they announced, would be given only when the three venerable sages had more time to reflect upon them.

"My great teacher, the Maggid, didn't need any time to answer these questions."

The Alter Rebbe stood up and objected, saying, "We agreed that before we began the second part of the debate, my questions would be answered.

Eighteen years ago, when I first came to my master and teacher, the Maggid, I asked him these three questions. Without hesitating a moment, he answered them all." The Alter Rebbe then repeated the Maggid's answers at great length, explaining them in such a clear and simple way that everyone was astounded.

He then took the opportunity to explain the basic philosophy of *Chassidus*.

One of his debaters and the majority of the *Bais Din* of Minsk declared that *Chassidus* was against the way of the Torah. They used the Alter Rebbe's refusal to continue the debate as the basis for their decision.

However, many of the scholars who were present, although remaining opposed to *Chassidus*, felt that the *Beis Din* had been too rash in its decision.

The *gaon* Reb Zemel, who was another one of the debaters, was also of this second opinion. When he mentioned his feelings to the *gaon* HoRav Chanoch Henoch, the latter agreed and then said, "My son Pinchas informed me that he has decided to become a chossid."

In addition to Reb Pinchas, Reb Yitzchok Isaac of Vitebsk,[36] a nephew of Reb Zemel, together with

---

36. Not to be confused with Reb Isaac Homiler.

another sixty young scholars, went to Liozna to become chassidim of the Alter Rebbe. Many more who had attended the debate stopped opposing *Chassidus* and developed a great respect for the Alter Rebbe.

COMING
TO THE
ALTER REBBE

To Reb Pinchas' surprise and delight, everyone in Shklov had heard of the debate and its outcome even before he arrived home. He was now hopeful that his decision to become a chossid would be accepted without causing an argument. However, what happened exceeded even his greatest expectations.

His mother-in-law Reizel was an extremely wealthy and charitable woman as well as being profoundly pious. For years she had only heard negative things about chassidim and their leaders. Now she heard how the young Maggid of Liozna had decisively won the debate vindicating *Chassidus* and its adherents. Their greatest scholars, the pride of the opposition, had failed even to approach the greatness of this Chassidic leader.

This intrigued her so much that she informed her three sons-in-law of the following: "Although until now we were all opposed to the new movement, in all truthfulness, I see we were mistaken. Therefore, I have decided that I will give my entire fortune to the one who goes to Liozna and becomes a student of the Maggid of Liozna."

Reb Pinchas had already informed his father of his decision to become a chossid of the Alter Rebbe. However, he had not yet acted upon his idea, as he wished to first discuss it with his wife. Thrilled that not only would it not create friction in the family, but it was being encouraged, he announced his willingness to go. [Some time later, one of his brothers-in-law joined him.][37]

He immediately set out on the journey and soon arrived in Liozna. However, for the next five months he had to satisfy himself by learning from the Alter Rebbe's chassidim. The Alter Rebbe was still traveling, attracting more and more followers. When the Alter Rebbe finally arrived back in Liozna, Reb Pinchas, after being thoroughly tested, was accepted into his second class.[38]

---

37. In *Beis Rebbe* it is mentioned that the name of this brother-in-law was Reb Zalman Reizes.

    We should note that Reb Zalman Reizes' son Reb Yaakov Kuli-Slonim married one of the Mitteler Rebbe's daughters, Rebbetzin Menucha Rochel.

    However, we should note that another one of his brothers-in-law was the chossid Reb Binyomin Kletzker.

38. To be accepted in the third class was a tremendous feat, as one had to be proficient in the entire *Shas (Talmud)* and the Rambam. To be accepted into the second class, one was tested on the other aspects of the Torah as well.

Eight months after he left, Reb Pinchas returned home. He had with him a note from the Alter Rebbe stating that he had studied with him personally for three months. His mother-in-law, true to her word, gave him her entire fortune.

Following the ways of our sages of not becoming a disciple of a *Tzaddik* for monetary gain, Reb Pinchas took the money he had received and gave it to the Alter Rebbe to do with it as he saw fit.

The Alter Rebbe *bentched* Reb Pinchas with material riches in addition to further success in Torah study.[39] Reb Pinchas asked to be blessed in a third matter as well (it is believed that he requested a blessing for a child), but the Alter Rebbe did not answer him.

It definitely would have been more prestigious for Reb Pinchas to be called by his father's last name as HoRav Chanoch Henoch was the Chief Rabbi of Shklov and recognized as a *gaon* by Jews throughout the entire region. However, in view of the fact that it was his mother-in-law Reizel who encouraged him to become a chossid, chassidim called him Rebbe Pinchas "Reizes."

His brother-in-law Reb Binyomin was so great that he was in the first class.

39. It seems that this time, the Alter Rebbe accepted the money. We must say that the story "All the Way" occurred at a different time.

A short time after Reb Pinchas was accepted into the *cheder*, the Alter Rebbe instructed him and Reb Moshe Vilenker, who also came to him at that time, to go to Reb Moshe Zalman Feldman. There, they were to learn the important role song plays in the development of a chossid, especially in connection to how it can arouse one's concentration in *davening*.

The Rebbe once again referred to the law in the *Mishnah* about the collar of an animal and explained that it hints to one's service to Hashem. The *Mishnah* asks: How can one drive out his animal soul? The *Mishnah* then mentions that just as there are various kinds of animals, so too, does the Evil Inclination come in various guises. And for each of these guises of the *yetzer hara* there is a distinctive form of Divine service. The common thrust among all of them is to elevate oneself through prayer. And the way to achieve this is by singing a *niggun* in the middle of *davening*.

A
FAITHFUL
STUDENT

Chassidus gives a Jew vitality in his service to Hashem, just as water gives life to vegetation. When a person is full of life and vitality, he doesn't keep it to himself. Rather, he shares it with others.

In the summer of 5545 (תקמ״ה-1785), two disciples of the Maggid, Reb Shlomo Karliner and Reb Zev (Velvel) Zhitomer, visited the Alter Rebbe. The Alter Rebbe reiterated his position that the best way to counter the *misnagdim* was by spreading the teachings of *Chassidus*.

After the visitors left, the Alter Rebbe's brother, the Maharil (Reb Yehudah Leib), dispatched Reb Pinchas and a few other young men from *Cheder Beis* to various towns in Lithuania. He also informed them, in the name of the Rebbe, of the nature of this mission.

Each one of them was to spend two months in their designated town. Their purpose was to arouse people to study *Chassidus* and follow in the ways of chassidim. Of course, this had to be done in utmost secrecy.

In the course of the year, the fruits of their work were visible. More young, outstanding scholars from the cream of the opposition arrived in Liozna and became faithful chassidim of the Alter Rebbe.

The following year other students were sent to different cities and once again their mission was crowned with success.

Reb Pinchas, having been a chossid for a few years, noticed that while chassidim lived with every word and teaching of the Rebbe, they recorded very little. Although we know of many of the Alter Rebbe's early teachings and sayings, they represent only a fraction of what he actually said. This is especially so with the teachings of the Baal Shem Tov and the Maggid.

Reb Pinchas saw that the Rebbe's words were pearls of wisdom which brought thousands to serve Hashem with enthusiasm. He envisioned how much more could be accomplished. He began to transcribe the Alter Rebbe's teachings, being careful to write down every *maamar Chassidus* he heard exactly as he heard it. In addition, he went to great lengths to record from elder chassidim the *maamarim* that were said by the Alter Rebbe before Reb Pinchas became a chossid or when he was not present. In this way, he could share the Rebbe's teachings by spreading them to as many people as possible. He also recorded their stories of the Maggid and the Baal Shem Tov.

The Mitteler Rebbe sought out Reb Pinchas and heard many of the Alter Rebbe's *maamarim* from him. Some of the Mitteler Rebbe's *maamarim* are based on them. One such *maamar* is based on what the Alter Rebbe said before the Mitteler Rebbe was born.[40]

When the Rebbe the Tzemach Tzedek compiled the *sefer Likkutei Torah* from the thousands of *maamarim* of the Alter Rebbe, the transcriptions of Reb Pinchas were one of his main resources.

Reb Pinchas was so exacting in his *hanochos* (transcriptions), that sometimes he left a blank space in middle of a paragraph to indicate that several words had been omitted. He understood the need to preserve the teachings and sayings of the Alter Rebbe and share them with others. He would illustrate this by saying that just as one is careful with pearls not to lose even one, so too, the Rebbe's words are pearls of wisdom and we must take the

---

40. *Sefer HaToldos* of the Alter Rebbe, p. 315. The significance of this is that even if the Alter Rebbe said it in the year between the Maggid's *histalkus* in 5533 (1772) and the birth of the Mitteler Rebbe the following year, it was still before the Alter Rebbe openly accepted the *Nesius*. He only accepted it after Rav Menachem Mendel Horodoker moved to *Eretz Yisroel*, when the Mitteler Rebbe was three years old.

utmost care with every word and nuance. Chassidim say[41] that the Alter Rebbe referred to Reb Pinchas as a cemented cistern that doesn't lose a drop.[42]

While the purpose of *Chassidus* is to reveal G-dliness in this physical world, the Rebbeim revealed it gradually. After the Alter Rebbe published the *Tanya,* the *Satan* claimed that such a revelation must be stopped. The Alter Rebbe was therefore arrested for fifty-three days, one day for each of the fifty-three chapters he wrote in *Likkutei Amarim, Tanya.*

It is known that there were times during his recitation of a *maamar Chassidus* that the Alter Rebbe would be overcome with such tremendous awe that amongst other things his voice would become almost inaudible. The reason for this is that *Chassidus* is a revelation of G-dliness, and when the revelation is so elevated, a person becomes detached from the physical. At those times, Reb Pinchas would bend over and listen to the holy words that the Alter Rebbe would utter in a very quiet voice. Later, to make sure that he was recording it properly, he would repeat the *maamar* to the Alter Rebbe and also repeat those words. Sometimes the Alter Rebbe would ask, "When did

---

41. *Sefer HaToldos* of the Alter Rebbe, p. 555.
42. *Avos* 2:9.

you hear me say that?" and Reb Pinchas would reply, "When the Rebbe's voice was almost inaudible." The Alter Rebbe then replied that it was indeed an exceptional thought which he must toil to understand.

In addition to being one of the foremost transcribers (and it is for that reason that one of the first *seforim* of the Alter Rebbe's *maamarim* that was printed is "The Transcriptions of Reb Pinchas"),[43] he also was the source of many of the stories of the Alter Rebbe's life.

The stories that we know of the Alter Rebbe's first few discussions with the sages of Shklov (printed in sections one, two and three of this biography) are all thanks to Reb Pinchas. The inspiring story (printed towards the end of this book) of how the Alter Rebbe cured hundreds of chassidim who had fallen ill — some deathly so — one *Simchas Torah* is taken from his notes. It was to him that the Mitteler Rebbe explained the essence of a *yechidus*. Many more incidents are culled from his writings as well.

The author of *Beis Rebbe* writes that the Mitteler Rebbe called Reb Pinchas "the General of chassidim" in whom the Rebbeim confided. Indeed, when the Alter Rebbe's daughter, Rebbetzin Devorah Leah decided to choose a *Beis Din* and

---

43. Published by *Kehot* in 5718 (1958).

exchange her life for her father's life, Reb Pinchas was one of the three chassidim chosen. And as we will mention later, it was Reb Pinchas whom the Alter Rebbe trusted and instructed to make sure that his son, Horav Dov Ber, the Mitteler Rebbe, would succeed him.

One more example that illustrates how esteemed Reb Pinchas was to the Alter Rebbe occurred in 5566 (תקס"ו-1806).

The Tzemach Tzedek, who was then only seventeen, was already writing his own original thoughts in *Chassidus*. The Alter Rebbe instructed his granddaughter,[44] Rebbetzin Chaya Mushka (the Tzemach Tzedek's wife), to bring him some of her husband's writings.

Not knowing which ones to bring, Rebbetzin Chaya Mushka brought him a large notebook which contained the Tzemach Tzedek's discourse entitled, *"Shoresh Mitzvas HaTefillah."*

The Alter Rebbe enjoyed this discourse immensely. He called in his brother Rav Yehudah Leib (the Maharil) and Reb Pinchas, saying that he was going to recite the blessing of *Shehecheyanu.* He wanted them to answer "Amen," for the Torah

---

44. She was the oldest daughter of the Mitteler Rebbe and married her first cousin, the Tzemach Tzedek. The Tzemach Tzedek was the only son of the Alter Rebbe's daughter Rebbetzin Devorah Leah.

states that a fact is established on the word of two witnesses.

The Alter Rebbe explained that he had just seen the writings of his grandson, Reb Menachem Mendel, [the Tzemach Tzedek], and that these writings demonstrate that *Toras HaChassidus* is continuing into the third generation. The Alter Rebbe then quoted the *possuk* which states that once the Torah is established for three generations it will remain forever.

The Alter Rebbe then stood up and said the blessing *Shehecheyanu*, reciting Hashem's name, and they answered "Amen."

That year, the Mitteler Rebbe's daughter, Rebbetzin Devorah Leah, married Reb Yekusiel Zalman, a grandson of Reb Levi Yitzchok of Berditchev. The *chassunah* took place in the city of Zholbin and it is referred to as "the Great *Chassunah*."

In his invitation to Reb Pinchas, HaRav Dovber writes, "Come and I will reveal to you secrets that were hidden until now.[45]

From these incidents we see that Reb Pinchas was the chossid who was included in the Rebbe's

---

45. The Frierdiker Rebbe writes that both the Alter Rebbe and the Mitteler Rebbe revealed only to Reb Pinchas numerous aspects. In addition, most aspects of their communal work went through him.

family in times of happiness and joy as well as during times of sacrifice and resolve.

Undoubtedly, Reb Pinchas is an example of a true chossid, one who is totally devoted to the Rebbe and spreads and disseminates the teachings and greatness of his Rebbe to others. Notwithstanding all of this, he was an extremely humble person.

PUBLICIZING THE ALTER REBBE'S GREATNESS

Although the *gaon* HoRav Henoch was upset with his son's decision to become a chossid, he and his son remained close.

Ten years later, in 5554 (1794), HoRav Henoch saw his son's handwritten copy of the Alter Rebbe's *Hilchos Talmud Torah*. Thinking that it was his son's own brilliant thoughts — as nowhere was it mentioned that it was a copy — HoRav Henoch derived much pleasure from it. His son, thought his proud father, though a chossid, was still growing in learning, and to a great extent.

When Reb Pinchas came home, his father apologized for going through his notes which had been left on the table. "But," he quickly added, "I derived a lot of pleasure from your original thoughts and the clarity with which they were presented; you make such difficult and complex subject matter seem so simple."

Then HoRav Henoch added, "I would like to publish it so that everyone can see your greatness."

**"My son, your thoughts are excellent;
I would like to publish them."**

Reb Pinchas was in a dilemma. His father was under the impression that these were his own original thoughts; obviously he did not realize that his manuscript was a copy of the Alter Rebbe's writings. He knew that his father would derive much happiness from its publication. Not wanting to deprive him of this satisfaction, but also not wanting to divulge the secret, Reb Pinchas simply replied, "I would rather not."

His father proudly thought that the refusal was due to his son's humility and replied, "In that case, I would publish it without mentioning the author's name." To this Reb Pinchas agreed.

HoRav Henoch immediately wrote an approbation praising both the scholar and the brilliance of the work and published four thousand copies.

The response was overwhelming, and that year alone the *sefer* was reprinted twice. When it was shown to the Vilna Gaon, he said in its praise, "Only a true *gaon* could write such a *sefer*."

It was not until a year later that everyone found out that the author was none other than the leader of the chassidim, the Alter Rebbe.

However, Reb Chanoch was not wrong. Although the *sefer* was not his son's, Reb Pinchas was definitely growing in his learning.

As busy as he was recording and publicizing the Alter Rebbe's teachings, implementing the Rebbe's communal activities, and taking care of his own personal responsibilities, Reb Pinchas had a schedule of learning *Nigleh* in depth for two hours every day.

The breadth of his knowledge is illustrated in the following episode:

Once, on a journey with the Alter Rebbe, they stopped into a *beis midrash* where many *misnagdim* were learning and conversing. At a distance from them, two *misnagdim*, who obviously considered themselves scholars, spoke quietly. One said to the other, "Although the Maggid of Liozna is a great scholar — as was his teacher, Reb DovBer, the Maggid of Mezritch — his teacher's teacher, the Baal Shem Tov, was an assistant to a *melamed*. Obviously, he was a simple person and definitely not qualified to be called a *talmid chocham*."

Although the Alter Rebbe was at the opposite end of the *shul* and they were speaking in low voices, the Alter Rebbe's keen hearing made it possible for him to hear this disrespectful comment.

Getting up from his place, he walked over to them and said, "I would like to repeat to you an explanation that I heard from my Master and Rebbe, the Maggid, who heard it from his Master and Rebbe, the Baal Shem Tov." He then expounded on a particular topic for a few hours.

Related Reb Pinchas, "The first part I was able to comprehend. But then the [Alter] Rebbe said, 'This is the way Abaya learns it; I will now repeat the explanation the way Rava explains it.' That explanation was so intricate and deep I could no longer follow it. When I looked at those two 'scholars,' I saw that they were so overwhelmed by the profundity of it, they just stood there in shock and bewilderment. It was obvious that they didn't even understand the *first* part of his talk.

"Nevertheless, even without understanding the content of what the Alter Rebbe said, they clearly recognized that the Baal Shem Tov's greatness in Torah surpassed that of all the scholars they had ever known."[46]

Sefer HaToldos

---

46. *Sippurim Nora'im.*

Printing
the Tanya

In 5555 (1795), Reb Pinchas went to the fair at Leipzig, Germany, with his brother-in-law the renowned chossid Reb Binyomin Kletzker.[47] Hearing that someone was selling copies of the Alter Rebbe's *kuntreisim,* as the *Tanya* was then called, they each bought one copy.

After studying it for a short time, they realized, to their utter dismay, that there were mistakes in these copies. They suspected the errors were purposefully inserted in order to discredit the Alter Rebbe and prove that chassidim lack the proper faith in Hashem.

Winning the confidence of the bookseller, Reb Pinchas confirmed his suspicions. The book dealer was indeed selling these forged copies in order to

---

47. We should note that whenever they were at these fairs, they would publicize to Jews from all different communities, the beauty of *Chassidus* and the greatness of the Alter Rebbe.

   In addition to bringing hundreds of *yidden* to become chassidim of the Alter Rebbe, they were also responsible for the *maskilim's* decision not to try to infiltrate the chassidim of the Alter Rebbe, as they realized that they wouldn't be successful.

fight the "holy war" against chassidim, and he prided himself on already having sold 150 copies!

The bookseller smiled and said, "These forged copies will help us fight the Chassidic movement."

Reb Pinchas and Reb Binyomin realized it would cost them a substantial amount of money to buy the remaining four hundred-fifty "copies," as they all were handwritten. Nevertheless, with chassidim, no sacrifice, money or otherwise, is too great when it comes to protect the honor of the Rebbe and *Chassidus*.

Holding on to this evidence, they publicly proved that the *kuntreisim* had been intentionally tampered with by some of the Alter Rebbe's opponents.

After seeing these severe misrepresentations of his thoughts, the Alter Rebbe agreed to publish the handwritten *kuntreisim* as a printed *sefer*. However, he wanted Reb Zusha and Reb Yehudah Leib HaCohen, two of the Maggid's great disciples, to give their approbations.

Once again, it was Reb Pinchas,[48] together with Reb Moshe Vilenker and Reb Yitzchok Moshe of Yas, who were entrusted by the Alter Rebbe to receive their approbations.

See The Tanya, Its Story and History, ch. 2.

---

48. As we will see at the end of the next chapter, Reb Pinchas was also instrumental in the publication of the Alter Rebbe's *Shulchan Aruch*.

Guaranteeing the Continuity

The Alter Rebbe refused to be under Napoleon's rule for even a moment. So when he heard that the French army was approaching, he quickly fled Liadi. Before leaving, however, he had his entire house burned to the ground to prevent Napoleon from obtaining anything that belonged to him.[49] The only things saved were those items that could be loaded up on the wagons and taken with them.

The devastation of the war was enormous. Tens of thousands of Jews were displaced, their houses burned, and their livelihoods destroyed. They were in desperate need of housing, food and employment.

After suffering major losses, the French began their retreat from Russia and the Alter Rebbe immediately set out to alleviate the Jews' plight.

---

49. Chassidim explain that the Alter Rebbe thought Napoleon practiced witchcraft, and if he had obtained anything that belonged to the Alter Rebbe, he would have used it to help him conquer Russia, or at least nullify the Alter Rebbe's *tefillos* against him.

Reb Pinchas was given the task of finding ways and opportunities for people to earn a livelihood.[50]

With the war coming to an end, people's hopes were high that their lives would once again return to normal. However, tragedy soon struck, and the Alter Rebbe was *nistalek* ten days after he was able to settle in the village of Piena. Chassidim were at a loss. Who would guide them in their service of Hashem and give them wise counsel and special *brochos* for their spiritual and physical needs?

Reb Pinchas uplifted their spirits by delivering the following message, which he either wrote and sent to all the Chassidic cities and towns or delivered in person by traveling to various cities:

"Two years ago, when I was at the *chassunah* of the Rebbe's granddaughter, Rebbetzin Devorah Leah, to Reb Yaakov Yisroel, the grandson of Reb Menachem Nochum of Chernobyl, the Rebbe called me over and said in the presence of his son, HaRav DovBer, the father of the bride, 'You should make sure that my son HaRav DovBer succeeds me [as Rebbe,] and the *pidyonos* be given to him and no one

---

50. The Alter Rebbe also petitioned the Russian government for land on which the Jews could establish new communities and earn a livelihood. The following year, in appreciation for the Alter Rebbe's assistance in defeating Napoleon, the government granted the land to the Alter Rebbe's son and successor, the Mitteler Rebbe. On that large tract of land the Mitteler Rebbe established twenty-two new communities for thousands of families.

else. I am telling you this because I know my son's nature and humility, and I know he won't make his greatness known.'

"The Rebbe continued, saying, 'Only my son HaRav DovBer has the proper deep and clear understanding of *Chassidus*.'

"Let us all remain faithful to the Rebbe," implored Reb Pinchas. "We should accept his son [as the next Rebbe] and the light of *Chassidus* will continue to shine."

Knowing that this was the wish of the Alter Rebbe, they willingly became chassidim of HaRav DovBer, who later became known as the Mitteler Rebbe.[51]

At the same time, Reb Pinchas rallied the chassidim to come to the assistance of *Beis HaRav* (the Rebbe's household).

Spurred on by the double tragedy that had befallen them, chassidim responded with an open hand. In spite of the gravity of their own personal

---

51. Why did they have to be instructed? After the Baal Shem Tov's *histalkus*, the Maggid of Mezritch succeeded him. Similarly, after the *histalkus* of the Maggid, HaRav Menachem Mendel Horodoker, and not the Maggid's son, became the next Rebbe. So unless it was known that the Mitteler Rebbe was to become Rebbe, the chassidim might not have assumed that one of the Rebbe's children would automatically become Rebbe. It would have been even more difficult for them to know since the Mitteler Rebbe would not have publicized his willingness to become Rebbe.

situation, they contributed the enormous sum of 35,000 rubles.

However, the Mitteler Rebbe felt it belonged to the entire *Beis HaRav*, and not just to him, so he wrote to Reb Pinchas (who had collected it with Reb Zalman Dubrovna), asking that Reb Pinchas, his brother-in-law Reb Zalman Reizes, and the chossid Reb Shlomo Freides divide the remaining two-thirds among the entire family.[52]

In order that *bnei Yisroel* would be able to continue to benefit from the Alter Rebbe's greatness, the Mitteler Rebbe and his brothers decided to print their father's *Shulchan Aruch* (and other *seforim*) for the first time almost immediately after the Alter Rebbe's *histalkus*. However, the expense involved was way beyond their means, particularly since they had just lost everything in the war.

It was Reb Pinchas who again rose to the occasion. He forwarded the entire amount necessary, and the *Shulchan Aruch* was published the following year.

---

52. The reason the Mitteler Rebbe took a third — much more than anyone else received — is that half of his portion was spent on building a new *beis midrash*. So he was ultimately left with much less than the sum he was originally given.

HIS HISTALKUS AND THE MITTELER REBBE'S ARREST

Reb Pinchas was *nistalek* in the town of Lubavitch.[53] The Mitteler Rebbe instructed the chassidim to mourn him properly, for the "General of the chassidim" had passed away. He left an enormous sum of money, 90,000 rubles, to be given for *tzedakah*.[54] He also instructed that 25 rubles be given to the chassidim to purchase *mashke* so that they might *farbreng* and comfort one another.

---

53. He was buried in the area that was designated for the Rebbe's family. This is evident from the fact that years later Reb Chaim Avrohom (the Alter Rebbe's second son) was buried next to him.

    It is interesting to note that after his passing, a halachic question arose. The *Chevra Kadisha* felt; being that he had no children (and he designated a large sum of money for charity), they could charge his estate a larger amount than normal for his burial. The extra money would be *tzedokah* helping to cover those who are unable to pay. However, the Mitteler Rebbe ruled they could only charge the regular amount.

54. *Beis Rebbe*, vol. 1, ch. 56. However, in *Shmuos V'Sipurim*, vol. 3, it is recorded that a list of *tzedakah* Reb Pinchas gave during his lifetime was found in his documents and it totalled 90,000 rubles.

The precise date of Reb Pinchas passing and his age at that time are not known. However, we can safely say that he was blessed to live a relatively long life, passing away at around seventy-six years of age.

This assumption is based on the following: As previously mentioned, Reb Pinchas first met the Alter Rebbe in the winter of 5531 (תקל״א-1770). Since Reb Pinchas was a member of the "early risers" — those who came to learn in the *Beis HaMidrash* by three in the morning — it is safe to assume that he was at least twenty years old at that time, especially as he was able to repeat to his father the lengthy explanations which the Alter Rebbe said that morning for the esteemed scholars of the city.

Since he was not blessed with children, all of Reb Pinchas' belongings were inherited by his father's family. Now, though his father, HoRav Henoch, did not agree with the ways of chassidim, he was also against the strong measures that the *misnagdim* took to oppose *Chassidus*. A few of his grandchildren, however, were staunch opponents of Chassidism. They each inherited some of the remaining belongings which were not specified to be given to others. Amongst those belongings was the letter of the Mitteler Rebbe mentioned previously. The nephew who inherited it translated it falsely and then used it to incriminate the Rebbe to the Russian authorities, thereby causing the Mitteler Rebbe's arrest in Tishrei of 5587 (תקפ״ז-1827).[55]

The government received the accusation against the Mitteler Rebbe in the summer of 5586 (תקפ״ו-1826). This fact leads us to say that Reb Pinchas passed away that year (or perhaps at most during the previous year). Once the inheritor found the letter, he informed the government of his "findings."

This was fifty-six years after Reb Pinchas' initial encounter with the Alter Rebbe.

If our assumption that he was around twenty at that time is correct, then he lived around seventy-six years.

Of course, it is possible that he was only around fifteen years old when he came to the Alter Rebbe and despite his young age, he was extremely studious and capable. If this is the case, then he only lived until the age of seventy. It is also possible that he was older than twenty when he first met the Alter Rebbe which would make him even more than seventy-six years at the time of his passing.

Whatever his age at his passing, Reb Pinchas' life was rich not only because of his monetary wealth,

---

55. He was subsequently freed six weeks later on *Yud Kislev*.
    According to recently published documents, the arrest began a year earlier in 5586 (1825).

but even more so because of his endearment to the Rebbeim and to the chassidim.

Although Reb Pinchas had no children, he left the chassidim a tremendous legacy. Many of the Alter Rebbe's *maamarim* and sayings which we find in the teachings of the Rebbeim are taken from his records. In addition, incidents and stories of the Alter Rebbe, the Mitteler Rebbe, and the growth of Chassidism were related and preserved by him for all generations. We are still benefiting from his greatness.

His Family

As mentioned, Reb Pinchas was not blessed with any children. However, in accordance with the spiritual interpretation of the *mitzvah p'ru u'r'vu* ("be fruitful and multiply"), Reb Pinchas "gave birth" to many, inspiring them to become connected to the Rebbeim and to serve Hashem according to the ways of *Chassidus*.

Reb Pinchas was especially instrumental in Shklov. Some of those affected were either related to him or became chassidim through his influence. The more famous of them were:[56]

Reb Zalman Reizes (the husband of his wife's sister). His son Reb Yosef Kuli Slonim married the Mitteler Rebbe's daughter, Rebbetzin Menucha Rochel, and later on they moved to *Eretz Yisroel*.

---

56. Subsequently all of these great chassidim inspired others in Shklov and elsewhere.

Just to mention a few: Rav Avrohom Shainess was inspired to become a chossid after listening to Reb Yosef Kolbo saying *Tikkun Chatzos*. Some years later he married the Alter Rebbe's youngest daughter Rebbetzin Rochel.

According to many, Reb Zalman Zezmer became a chossid after hearing Reb Binyomin Kletzker saying the *parshah* of *Mechias Amalek*. He in turn influenced Reb Hillel Paritcher to become a *Chabad* chossid.

When the Mitteler Rebbe was arrested in Vitebsk, they also arrested Reb Zalman.

Reb Isser Kisis, one of Reb Zalman's brothers.

Reb Binyomin Kletzker, renowned for becoming completely immersed in the teachings of *Chassidus* — even when he was in the middle of his business dealings. He was a partner and relative of Reb Pinchas.

Among the great chassidim of Shklov influenced by Reb Pinchas were:

Reb Yosef Kolbo, who originally taught Reb Pinchas.

Reb Shlomo Freides, whose daughter married the Rebbe the Tzemach Tzedek's son the Maharil.

Reb Zalman Rivlin and his brother Reb Leib.

FAITH IN
TZADDIKIM[57]

25.

This is the story, as Reb Pinchas [Reizes] of Shklov recounted it to my great-great-uncle, Reb Nachum.[58]

* * *

That year, 5547 (תקמ״ז; 1786), winter set in with a vengeance, and Liozna[59] had its first snowfall during *Chol HaMoed* Sukkos. It was bitterly cold, and to be able to sit in the *sukkah* people had to put on fur coats and padded boots. Besides, some of the meals there could not start until the snow had been cleared from the roof. That year Shemini Atzeres fell on *Shabbos*. Snow fell all Friday night, and in the morning the Alter Rebbe asked someone to remark

---

57. Reprinted from the English translation of *Likkutei Dibburim*, vol. II, chapter 14, pp. 161-176, and therefore we didn't change the section numbers of the chapters. The Frierdiker Rebbe said this story on the 25th of Shevat 5696 (תרצ״ו; 1936).
58. Reb Nachum was the Mitteler Rebbe's oldest son.
59. Liozna was the home of the Alter Rebbe from 1767 to 1801. He then settled in Liadi from 1801-1813.

to Kuzma,[60] the gentile handyman, that it would be impossible to eat in the *sukkah* as long as the snow

Kuzma goes to clear away the snow.

---

60. Remark to Kuzma: An explicit instruction would have constituted a desecration of the holy day.

was piled up on top. He duly cleared the snow away, and the Rebbe went out to the *sukkah* to recite the *Kiddush* and eat the festive meal of *Shabbos* and *Yom-Tov* there.

Most of the chassidim who had converged on Liozna for Shemini Atzeres and Simchas Torah suffered from frozen fingers and toes, and many of them had caught heavy colds.

Now on Hoshanah Rabbah,[61] it was the Rebbe's custom to have all the *Sifrei Torah* taken out of the Holy Ark and properly rolled together again, and bound in such a way that the row of stitches which joined any two neighboring sheets of parchment would fall exactly halfway between the wooden roller *(etz chaim)* on either side. The scrolls were then carefully tied with their binders.

Reb Michel the *shammes* was most punctilious that everything to do with the *shul* should be done precisely, promptly, and calmly. The person who received the instruction from the Rebbe's mouth traditionally supervised the *shammes* and the few chassidim who helped him in this task, and when it was completed he would enter the Rebbe's study to report that the *Sifrei Torah* were properly tied up.

And that year it was my privilege to be honored by the Rebbe with this responsibility.

---

61. On *Hoshanah Rabbah:* i.e., the day before the dancing of *Shemini Atzeres* and *Simchas Torah.*

26.

Hoshanah Rabbah that year fell on Friday. The Rebbe was of cheerful countenance, so when I had informed him that my task was completed, I made mention[62] of the chassidim who had caught heavy colds on the way to town, and many of whom were running a high fever.

The Rebbe leaned his head on his arms, lapsed into a state of *dveikus* for quite some time, then opened his eyes and said in his characteristic singsong: "Concerning the Torah it is written, אש דת למו — that it is 'a fiery law for them.'[63] Now today is Simchas Torah. So let them all be brought along for the *Hakkafos*, for [in the *Gemara* the Divine Presence is referred to as] אש אוכלת אש — 'one fire that consumes another fire.'[64] The fire of Simchas Torah will consume the fire of their fever."[65]

Now in Liozna at that time there lived two aged scholars who had been amongst the earliest *misnagdim*. True indeed they had the greatest respect for the Alter Rebbe, but nevertheless they were *misnagdim* through and through. One of them

---

62. Made mention: In the Heb./Yid. original מזכיר געווען; signifies a request that the Rebbe intercede on behalf of the individual named.
63. A fiery law: *Devarim* 33:2.
64. One fire...another fire: *Tractate Yoma* 21b.
65. The fire of their fever: Lit., "...of their cold."

was known as Reb Aizik Mechadesh[66] (מחדש), and the second as Reb Naftali Zahir (זהיר). Both of them indeed were exceedingly learned, and both of them were exceedingly G-d-fearing. Reb Aizik was always announcing: "Today, thanks to the Almighty, I was *mechadesh* such and such in the Torah." That was how he acquired his nickname. As to Reb Naftali, he was forever proclaiming: "I am scrupulously vigilant (Heb.: *zahir*) as to what I eat; I am scrupulously vigilant as to what I say; I am scrupulously vigilant as to where I look; I am scrupulously vigilant in this, that and the other." And that was how he acquired *his* nickname.

These two scholars had both been students at the *yeshivah* of Smilevitz, which had been famous fifty or sixty years beforehand, when it was headed by a saintly sage called Reb Shalom Yudel. To him the Prophet Eliyahu had revealed himself on a number of occasions, and he had produced a number of outstanding students. By the time Reb Aizik and Reb Naftali had arrived at the yeshivah this sage was old and blind, and the *shiurim* (Torah lessons) were delivered by his second son-in-law, Reb

---

66. *Mechadesh:* Verb signifying the scholarly achievement of hitting upon a novel analysis or conclusion in the course of *Talmudic* debate.

Shimon Eliyahu, who was known as "the *ilui* (genius) of Drutzin."[67]

In fact before my father[68] was married he studied under him for quite a period, at a time when his mentor had already been the senior *rosh yeshivah* of Smilevitz for over twenty years.

"It was such a delight to hear Reb Shimon Eliyahu propounding a *chiddush*," my father would recall, "that you didn't feel the passage of time. And when he delivered a *pilpul* you could feel his arguments sweeping through the air, and your head would ache from their sheer profundity."

27.

When my father[69] by intellectual compulsion began to find himself on the side of the Alter Rebbe, and began to develop a strong liking for the teachings of *Chassidus*, he would often say: "I am certain that if Reb Shimon Eliyahu would only have heard the sheer depth of Divine wisdom that is to be found in *Chassidus*, he would certainly have become a chossid. And if he had invested his mighty talents in its teachings, and expounded its

---

67. This was a village near Kochanov, in the Mohilev region, and Reb Shimon Eliyahu was born into one of the ten or so families of Jewish farmers who lived there.
68. Reb Pinchas' father, Reb Chanoch Henoch.
69. This is one of the basis to say although Reb Chanoch Henoch did not become a chossid, he distanced himself from the *misnagdim*.

explanations with his eloquent tongue, the greatest scholars would have become chassidim."

At any rate, Reb Aizik Mechadesh was a native of Optzug and Reb Naftali Zahir hailed from Kochanov, and fifty years earlier they had both married and settled in Liozna, where they had been enabled by their wealthy fathers-in-law to continue as lifelong students.

People used to relate that when the Alter Rebbe arrived in Liozna for the first time and delivered a *pilpul*,[70] Reb Aizik was immensely impressed. In fact he and Reb Naftali agreed that since the days when the *ilui* (genius) of Drutzin used to deliver his fortnightly *pilpul* to an audience of the most distinguished scholars, they had never heard another like it.

When the Alter Rebbe later settled in Liozna, the two elderly scholars often consulted him on *halachic* questions, and after each such learned discussion they were left open-mouthed.

28.

At this time the townsmen of Liozna, like the townspeople from the surrounding districts, were *misnagdim* in all their ways, yet they were different from the *misnagdim* in the regions of Vilna, Minsk, Brisk and Slutzk.

---

70. *Pilpul:* A finely honed legalistic argumentation.

The old folk of Vitebsk and Mohilev and the surrounding townships used to describe how in those days one would often encounter various passersby who would drop into a local *beis midrash* and tell their listeners stories of a certain sage and *tzaddik* who lived in the region of Podolia; he was always exerting himself to better the lot of his brethren and was a worker of great miracles. These passersby included eminent scholars who were at home in the entire *Talmud,* and they would liken the miracles recounted of this *tzaddik* of Podolia to the miracles recorded in the *Talmud* of various *tannaim* and *amoraim.*

In those days people did not know who these passersby were, but in our time, when we were with the Rebbe in Liozna, we knew that they were *tzaddikim nistarim,* hidden saints, the colleagues and disciples of the Baal Shem Tov, and they used to travel about the countryside in order to tell the masses about the Baal Shem Tov and about his teachings on Divine service.

A few years elapsed until the ban on the teachings of the Baal Shem Tov was first proclaimed at the fair of the regional councils of Vilna and Slutzk. The typical scholar or householder did not understand the point of the councils' prohibitions; in fact they enjoyed listening to the beautiful stories of these learned wanderers. Because the regions of

Vitebsk and Mohilev were inhabited by simple G-d-fearing townsfolk and scholars, they were the first to become chassidim, and the *misnagdim* of those parts were also different from the *misnagdim* in the regions of Vilna, Brisk, Slutzk and Shklov.

29.

One day, when the Alter Rebbe had returned to Liozna after his first visit to [the Maggid of] Mezritch, Reb Aizik and Reb Naftali asked him why he had gone to the trouble of traveling all the way to the province of Volhynia, especially since this entailed a certain wastage of time from Torah study. After all, Vilna was much closer, and he could have clarified any of his scholarly queries by visiting "Reb Elinke *Gaon*" (i.e., Reb Eliyahu, the *Gaon* of Vilna).

To this the Alter Rebbe replied: "In Vilna one learns how a Jew should study Torah, whereas in Mezritch one learns how the Torah teaches a Jew — until he himself becomes a Torah."

In the years during which the Alter Rebbe began to reveal and disseminate the teachings of the Baal Shem Tov and the Maggid of Mezritch, Reb Aizik and Reb Naftali grew apart from him, though they continued to treat him with the greatest respect.

There had been a time when the Alter Rebbe's distinguished brothers — Reb Yehudah Leib, Reb

Mordechai and Reb Moshe — had come to Liozna, and the Alter Rebbe had delivered an advanced *shiur* in *Gemara* for their benefit three times a week, following the mode of study characteristic of the *Rishonim*. Reb Aizik and Reb Naftali had then been numbered among the select scholars who were also present at those sessions. Moreover, in the year 5536 (תקל"ו-1776), when the Alter Rebbe founded the first *cheder* and mapped out a course of study for the married students who were arriving in Liozna, under the supervision of his learned brothers, Reb Aizik and Reb Naftali would often walk into the white *beis midrash* in order to listen and discuss. Later, however, when the Alter Rebbe began expounding Chassidic teachings in public, the two local scholars grew distant from him.

Yet though they opposed the ways of the Baal Shem Tov, and even more so the teachings of the Baal Shem Tov and the Maggid, they still held the Alter Rebbe in the highest esteem. So much so, in fact, that when in the year 5539 (תקל"ט-1779) the regional council of Slutzk published its ban against the Alter Rebbe and against *Chassidus*, and news of this reached Liozna, Reb Aizik and Reb Naftali signed a letter of protest in which they testified that the Alter Rebbe was a *gaon* and a *tzaddik*. Throughout that period, however, they still had their reservations about miracles.

30.

Now Reb Aizik's brother had a son called Reb Moshe Optzuger, who was a chossid of the Alter Rebbe. For the above-mentioned Simchas Torah[71] he came to Liozna accompanied by two sons and a son-in-law, and all four guests lodged together in the home of Reb Aizik. Reb Moshe was a man of weak constitution, and after the ordeal of the arduous trek in the fierce cold he was kept in bed by a very high fever. His sons and son-in-law also fell ill. Avraham the Doctor said that with G-d's help the younger men would somehow find their way out of their illness alive. As to Reb Moshe, however, old and weak as he was, and with pains in both sides and high fever too, he was very doubtful if he would survive.

Reb Aizik was deeply distressed and complained constantly that the whole idea of traveling to see one's Rebbe in such conditions was a *mitzvah* earned at the expense of a transgression.[72]

31.

After *Maariv* on the eve of Shemini Atzeres, I and a fellow townsman by the name of Ephraim Michel and Chaim Elye[73] of Dubrovna took along

---

71. The above-mentioned Simchas Torah: In 1786; see above, Section 25.
72. Mitzvah...expense of a transgression: Hence forbidden; in the original, הבאה בעבירה (Tractate *Berachos* 47b).
73. Elye: Affectionate diminutive form of Eliyahu.

quite a number of young men, and set out for all the local hostelries, in order to invite — or, if need be, to bring — all the out-of-town guests to *shul* for *Hakkafos,* so that they should all be warmed and healed by the fire of the Torah.

As we arrived at each inn, I told the chassidim there what the Rebbe had said. In fact his words were already known, because as soon as I had left the Rebbe's study I had walked into the little shul in the courtyard and had told everyone there what I had said to the Rebbe about those who were sick, and what the Rebbe had answered. Within an hour, word of this had reached all the inns in town. Nevertheless, as I arrived at each one, the lodgers there asked me to repeat the Rebbe's words, letter by letter.

It was a veritable delight to see the joy that the Rebbe's words aroused in each hostelry, among the women and children too, for now everyone was certain that with G-d's help all the patients would recover.

That was a tempestuous night indeed — a night of sleet, torrents of rain, and a wind that went right through your bones. The streets, moreover, were one great quagmire. But none of this prevented the sick from going to *shul* Many were able to walk alone, except for a little support on the side; others, who were unable to walk, we had to carry.

When we arrived at the house of Reb Aizik, we found him arguing with the sons and son-in-law of his nephew Reb Moshe. The three young men were arguing that they wanted a message to be sent to our little party [who had been expected at any minute] that we should come and help them stumble their way to *Hakkafos*, and carry Reb Moshe there too. Reb Aizik argued that it was unthinkable that even they should go out of doors. As for their father Reb Moshe, there was nothing even to discuss, for since daytime he had lain in a stupor, oblivious to the world. In fact Avraham the Doctor had said that his life was in danger. If he were to be carried outdoors, the first gust of wind would whisk him out of the land of the living, G-d forbid.

32.

When Chaim Elye Dubrovner and I and another couple of young fellows entered on the scene, Reb Moshe's sons were so overjoyed that they cried out: "Thank G-d! Now we are all saved, our father and all of us!"

"Murderers, that's what you are!" shouted Reb Aizik. "What you're doing is an offense against the holy Torah!"

I approached Reb Moshe. He was lying still as a log, his skin dark and bluish, his eyes closed. He was in high fever.

"Reb Moshe was lying still as a log, his skin dark and bluish, his eyes closed. He was in high fever."

I took such fright that I almost lost my wits.

Reb Aizik turned to us: "What do you say? This dangerously ill patient they want to take to *shul* for *Hakkafos?!* Even when the *Beis HaMikdash* was standing, and even when people were already in Jerusalem, the *Gemara* in Tractate *Chagigah*[74] teaches

---

74. Tractate *Chagigah:* 1:1.

us explicitly [regarding the obligatory pilgrimage]: תנו רבנן, שלש רגלים, פרט לחיגר ולחולה — '...except for the lame and the sick.' Surely, then, this limitation applies to a *mitzvah* instituted by the Sages. If you carry Moshe outdoors now, you will be guilty of outright murder!"

But then Chaim and Baruch, Reb Moshe's sons, spoke up. Since the Rebbe had said that this was a cure, they believed with perfect faith that if their father were carried off to the *minyan* for the Rebbe's *Hakkafos* he would recover.

I must confess that at that moment I was confused and didn't know what to say. On the one hand, I heard Reb Aizik's arguments and watched Reb Moshe lying there, his very life flickering. On the other hand, I could hear the words of simple faith spoken by his sons — homespun villagers, one a tailor and the other a merchant, and it was they in whom the faith in a *tzaddik* radiated to the very point of self-sacrifice, without any prior meditation whatever.

Mortal reason dictated that Reb Aizik was of course right. A patient in this state should obviously not be moved from his bed. The slightest draft would endanger his life; if they were to take him out in such a storm, they might never get him as far as the *beis midrash*, G-d forbid. But then the Divine reason clothed in the G-dly soul argued that

Chaim and Baruch were right. If the Rebbe said that the fire of the Torah was a cure, then it was a cure, and one ought to stake one's life on it.

33.

Moment by moment I was more amazed by Reb Moshe's sons — ordinary young men with earnest hearts. To this very day I recall the shame that welled up within me. I felt so humbled that I resolved that I really ought to speak to the Rebbe at *yechidus*.

"Here I am," I told myself, "Pinchas the son of HoRav Henoch of Shklov,[75] who was privileged to study *Gemara* and *poskim* and Torah philosophy[76] at the feet of Shklov's mightiest sages; who has come to appreciate the stature of the Rebbe through the comprehension of his teachings; who is now enjoying my eighth year in his presence; — and *still* the Matter in me prevails over the Form, and the natural intelligence prevails over the intelligence of the soul; while these simple young men, who came here to the Rebbe only out of a G-d-fearing sense of duty, and who do not comprehend the profundity of the Rebbe's teachings, — in them the Form prevails over the Matter, and the intelligence of the soul radiates within them in an experience of simple

---

75. Pinchas . . . of Shklov: In the more picturesque original, "Pinye Reb Henoch's Shklover."
76. Torah philosophy: In the original, חקירה.

faith! Be ashamed of yourself, Pinye Reb Henoch's! Be ashamed in the presence of this chassidisher village tailor, in the presence of that chassidisher village merchant!"

So deep was I in my reverie that I did not notice what was going on around me — until Chaim Elye Dubrovner nudged me and said: "Avraham the Doctor says that the poor old man is in his last hours, G-d forbid."

I had not yet managed to take stock of the situation, when I heard Baruch calling out aloud: "Father! The Rebbe has sent messengers to invite you to come to *Hakkafos*! Father, wake up! We have to go to the Rebbe's *Hakkafos*!"

There was a whole uproar in his room. When I walked in I saw Reb Moshe lying there with his eyes open, a smile on his face, and waiting to be taken along to the Rebbe's *beis midrash*. Chaim Elye darted out to call in another few young chassidim while others dressed Reb Moshe, who was unable to move a limb alone, and then he was lifted and carried off to the Rebbe's *minyan* for *Hakkafos*.

34.

As we walked into the big *shul* in the courtyard, the heat struck us in the face. The *minyan* was packed from wall to wall with people. Some of them were so sick that they could not even sit on the benches and had to be propped up against the walls. They at least were quiet, but others coughed without respite, or groaned so pitifully that one's heart was sore at the sight.

The most serious case there was Reb Yaakov Yeshayahu of Chotemsk. He was in his sixties, charitable and hospitable, a scholar and a *baal avodah*,[77] who worked as a *melamed* from time to time, and ran a modest hostelry. In the course of the years he had several times made his way on foot to visit the Maggid of Mezritch; he had then gone[78] to Horodok a couple of times; and after Reb Menachem Mendel had left for *Eretz Yisrael*[79] he had instead visited the Alter Rebbe, among whose chassidim he was regarded as a man with a seasoned understanding of *Chassidus*. Physically, he was so tall and well-built that his friends used to nickname him "Yaakov Yeshayahu *Kohen Gadol*" ("High Priest," but lit., "the big *Kohen*"). According to Avraham the Doctor, this man's very strength had made him so vulnerable, though he predicted that in the long run his strength would enable him to ward off the Angel of Death. For the moment, nevertheless, he lay there prone and listless, a mighty ruin that was awesome to behold.

---

77. *Baal avodah:* A person who seriously engages in Divine service, particularly through prayer and (in Chassidic usage) through the labor of self refinement.
78. He had then gone: The Maggid had passed away in 1772.
79. Had left for *Eretz Yisrael:* In 1777.

35.

On the afternoon of Hoshanah Rabbah, on the eve of Shemini Atzeres, it was customary to pray early, in the Rebbe's little *minyan* that was known among the chassidim as "the Lower Garden of Eden" — at the same time that *Minchah* was begun on the eve of Yom Kippur. Straight after *Minchah*, the light of joy was already in the air, and you could often hear the Rebbe studying alone in his room. Later in the afternoon the Rebbe would deliver a discourse to the scholars of the chadarim and to a select company of guests.

A couple of hours later it was time for *Maariv* in the Rebbe's little *minyan,* and after this the Rebbe would begin *Hakkafos* together with a certain number of the scholars of the *chadarim* and of the guests from out of town. The Rebbe himself would recite aloud all the verses of *Atah hareisa,* lead all of the seven circuits around the *bimah,* and read aloud all the accompanying hymns and verses. Every time he walked around that table, he would leave his spot at the south-eastern corner of the *shul,* advance towards the south-west, pause a moment to hold the *Sefer Torah* in his left hand, rest his right hand on the shoulder of one of the elder chassidim — and with him he would dance.

While this was going on, the chassidim present literally experienced illumination; every man there felt that he was standing at the site of the *Beis HaMikdash*; every instant was precious beyond compare; it now seemed within everyone's reach to clamber to the loftiest heights of Torah, *avodah*, and repentance; at this moment they experienced the ideal described by the Sages: משם היו שואבין רוח הקודש — "From these wellsprings[80] they drew Divine inspiration."

Whoever was fortunate enough to be present at "the Rebbe's *yechidus-Hakkafos*" — to behold that face, that Holy of Holies; to hear those songs of joy; to witness that dance of bliss; to see reflected in all of this an outpouring of a rapturous love of G-d; — such a man felt that he too was caught up in the splendor of the innermost Sanctuary that filled the very air of that little *shul*.

36.

These *Hakkafos* were known among chassidim as "the Rebbe's *yechidus-Hakkafos*," for at this time the most subtle, innermost facet of the soul — the *makkif* of the *yechidah* — revealed itself. Moreover, this was one of the most propitious times for the "nearing of the luminary to the spark."[81]

It is clear in the minds of chassidim that the conduct of the Rebbe echoes the proceedings on

---

80. From these wellsprings: *Ruth Rabbah* 4:10.
81. Luminary. . . spark: In the original, קרוב המאור אל הנצוץ; here serves as an analogy for Rebbe and chassid.

high. When there is an auspicious time on high, and the Countenance of the celestial King is radiant, so too is it an auspicious time with the Rebbe, and his countenance too is radiant.

The Rebbe's *yechidus-Hakkafos* used to give a chassid a firm footing at an utterly new level. I remember that my first time there triggered off a whole turmoil within me. I became a new man. It was then, for the first time, that I was able to picture how a Jew used to feel when he made the festive pilgrimage to the *Beis HaMikdash,* and there saw the Divine Presence revealed.

* * *

Every organ has its own distinctive pleasure, in harmony with its own nature. The head derives pleasure from thinking, the eyes from seeing, the ears from hearing, the heart from traits of noble character, the hand from action and the foot from walking, and so on. But there exists a kind of bliss that is experienced simultaneously by the whole man, to the point that all his faculties, senses and gifts lose their identity within it. And just such a bliss was the lot of every chassid who took part in the Rebbe's *yechidus-Hakkafos.*

* * *

Just as in the laws of the *Beis HaMikdash* and its vessels every detail is precisely ordered and regulated in terms of time and place, so too in the Rebbe's precincts the time and place of every activity was defined — in regulations that all the chassidim knew and punctiliously observed, for they were all devoted to the Rebbe with all their heart, soul and might.

Thus, for example, everyone knew that the Rebbe's *yechidus-Hakkafos* ought to be attended only by those named by the person in charge. Everyone, to be sure, prayed that he should have the good fortune to be named, but one would never go there without being invited. And having once participated, one would never again be allowed to join in, except for the Rebbe's close relatives and a few other chassidim.

37.

After the *yechidus-Hakkafos* the Alter Rebbe would go into the *sukkah* to recite *Kiddush*, and then proceed to the big shul in the courtyard for *Hakkafos*.

But something unusual happened that year. When the Rebbe entered the *sukkah* for *Kiddush*, he asked that three chassidim be called to him — Reb Michael Aharon of Vitebsk, Reb Shabsai Meir of Beshenkovitz, and Reb Yaakov of Semilian.

To Reb Michael Aharon, the Rebbe said, "You are a *Kohen*"; to Reb Shabsai Meir he said, "You are a *Levi*"; and to Reb Yaakov he said, "You are a *Yisrael*."

The Rebbe then addressed all three: "I need a rabbinical court of three, which needs to comprise a *Kohen*, a *Levi*, and a *Yisrael*, and that is why I have chosen you to constitute this *beis din*. You shall now listen to *Kiddush*, and after each of its blessings you are to respond 'Amen,' remembering that the assent that this signifies is to apply to all the spiritual intentions and the requests that I shall have in mind."

Before proceeding, the Rebbe asked for several large wine vessels. Then, having recited *Kiddush*, he poured the wine that remained in his goblet into one of the vessels, and told the three members of the *beis din* that he now appointed them to be "emissaries of healing."[82] They were to mix the wine from the first vessel, into which he had poured, with the wine in the other vessels, and distribute it among the sick, who would then be completely cured. They were to go upstairs to the women's gallery as well, and pour wine for those women who had never been blessed with children or who had miscarried.

Word spread in a flash that whoever tasted this wine would be healed of all his ailments, and that

82. Emissaries of healing: In the original, *sheluchei refuah*.

women who were childless or who had miscarried
would be helped from Above. The *beis din* of three
meanwhile selected a squad of young chassidim to
carry and distribute the wine. Among them were
Ephraim Michl, Shemaya Berl's, Zalman Mottel's,
Elya Avraham's and Yeshaya Nota's, all from
Shklov; Chaim Elya, Shimon Baruch's, Avraham

**"Answer *Amen*, not only to the blessing
but also to everything I shall have in mind."**

Zalman's and Leib Yitzchak, all from Dubrovna; Avraham Abba from Rudny; Yehoshua from Horodok; Zelig from Kochanov; Gedaliah from Kalisk; Berl Meir, Yosef Avraham, Tuvia Meilech's and Moshe Hirsch, all from Vitebsk; and Aharon Yosef, Shmuel Moshe and Yisrael, all from Liozna.

Among the circles of the burly young men of the time, each of the above-mentioned stalwarts enjoyed a reputation (May no Evil Eye befall it!) for his brawn rather than his brain.[83]

38.

As soon as the three members of the *beis din* entered the big shul in the courtyard, silence fell on all those present. Everyone knew that these were the chosen men whom the Rebbe had appointed as emissaries of healing and salvation, and gazed upon them in reverent awe. The *beis din* together with some of their helpers stepped up to the *bimah*, and Reb Yaakov of Semilian repeated the Rebbe's words aloud, letter by letter.

As he concluded he said: "Thus far is what the Rebbe said. Now I would like to add a few words that are relevant to us now.

"There is a strong tradition, handed down from one generation of elders to the next, that in order for

---

83. His brawn rather than his brain: In the original, גבורתם קודמת לחכמתם.

the blessing of a Rebbe to be realized, the person being blessed has to fulfill two conditions: firstly, that he should believe in the blessing with simple faith, without any alternative thought; secondly, that he should be ready and willing to carry out faithfully the desire of the *tzaddik* who gives the blessing, in matters of Divine service — whether in Torah study, in worship, or in ethical conduct."

Even though everyone heard the elder chassid clearly, nevertheless to be doubly sure they asked Reb Michael Aharon HaKohen, because his voice was louder, to repeat his words. And when that was over, the young men began in an orderly fashion to share out the Rebbe's wine.

39.

As the Rebbe came in for *Hakkafos* there was a hushed silence. For this second series it was his custom to read aloud the first verse[84] (אתה הראת לדעת) and the last verse[85] (כי מציון), and he would take a *Sefer Torah* for the circuit of the first and seventh *Hakkafah*.

The next day everyone was talking about the miracle. In fact Reb Avraham the Doctor said that for many of the elderly patients, this was a virtual resurrection of the dead; medically speaking, they

---

84. The first verse: *Devarim* 4:35; *Siddur*, p. 335.
85. The last verse: *Isa.* 2:3; *Siddur*, p. 336.

had been beyond all hope, and only through supernatural intervention had they been saved.

As for Reb Aizik, the miraculous recovery of his nephew Reb Moshe turned him into a chossid.

He later recalled: "The uncomplicated faith in a *tzaddik* which I saw then in my brother's grandchildren astounded me. I would never have believed it possible — unless I had seen it with my own eyes."

Reb Aizik had always been a profound and assiduous scholar, and these traits he now extended to the study of *Chassidus*. He repeatedly reviewed every *maamar* that the Rebbe delivered publicly, inquiring as to the meaning of its every word until he had the concept firmly in his grasp.

THE ESSENCE OF A YECHIDUS

This story was included here to show an aspect of the special relationship that existed between Reb Pinchas Reizes and the Mitteler Rebbe. On this particular occasion, the Mitteler Rebbe chose to reveal a very profound secret with no one but Reb Pinchas.

In the midst of a trip embarked upon one summer, the Mitteler Rebbe stopped at an inn not far from the city of Smargon. The summer weather was so beautiful that the Rebbe decided to stay there for a week.[86] As soon as the chassidim in the neighboring cities and towns heard that the Rebbe was staying in the area, they left their homes almost immediately and traveled to him.

In addition to saying *Chassidus* for all those assembled there, the Mitteler Rebbe accepted them in *yechidus*. One by one, each of the hundreds of chassidim spoke privately with the Rebbe and he answered their most pressing and personal questions concerning their service of Hashem, and matters of family, health and livelihood.

---

86. We can assume it was both for health reasons and making himself available to the chassidim there.

One day, as one of the chassidim was leaving from his *yechidus* in the Rebbe's room, the Mitteler Rebbe instructed his *gabbai* to stop the line. He would not be taking in anyone else into *yechidus* for the time being.

Although the hundreds of people who were still standing on line were understandably disappointed, they assumed this was only a temporary delay and *yechidus* would resume in a few hours. After all, they reasoned, the Rebbe had already seen hundreds of people the previous day and *yechidus* this day had already begun several hours ago. Surely the Rebbe was exhausted from hearing everyone's woes and needed a break.

They continued their preparations to see the Rebbe either by saying *Tehillim*, reviewing one of the Rebbe's latest *maamarim* or meditating on various explanations on *Chassidus*.

Half an hour later, the *gabbai*, Reb Zalman, left the antechamber of the Rebbe's room looking completely distraught, his eyes red from crying.[87] The chassidim followed his every move as he approached the elder chassidim and whispered something in their ears. Seeing the color drain from their faces, the chassidim were really alarmed. The

---

87. Reb Zalman had never heard the Mitteler Rebbe saying *Tehillim* with such an outpouring of emotion and assumed that something very dire must have occurred. Not knowing what it was, Reb Zalman himself began crying in fear.

Mitteler Rebbe was not merely resting. Something extremely serious was going on here!

After some time had passed, the elder chassidim made the decision to enter the house. Standing quietly outside the Mitteler Rebbe's door, they heard him pouring out his soul with words of *Tehillim* and crying from the depths of his heart as was done only on the most solemn days of the year.

Some of them fainted in anguish. Others cried out in pain. On a regular weekday in the month of Av, what could possibly cause the Rebbe to interrupt *yechidus* and begin saying *Tehillim* with such intensity?

Hearing about all that had transpired in the house, the crowds of chassidim became even more alarmed and formed *minyanim* to say *Tehillim* from the depths of their hearts. With each passing moment, their *Tehillim* grew in urgency, and tears flowed freely as they poured out their souls.

Meanwhile, in the Rebbe's room, a few hours had passed before the Rebbe concluded saying the entire *Tehillim*, and he then prepared himself to *daven Mincha*. However, he first had to lie down for over an hour to regain some of his strength since he had become worn out from saying *Tehillim* with such emotion.

When the chassidim heard that the Rebbe was *davening Mincha* with the same tune and devotion as he *davened* during the Ten Days of Repentance, they decided to *daven* as if it were a fast day.[88] In truth, many of them were fasting anyway as a preparation for entering *yechidus*.

After *Mincha*, the Rebbe went outside, stood on a makeshift platform in order to be better heard, and said a lengthy *maamar* on the topic of *teshuvah*. He explained that tears of *teshuvah* wash away improper speech and thoughts. He then pointed out the greatness of saying words of Torah and reciting *Tehillim*.

The Rebbe's words touched them very deeply and caused a great arousal amongst them. For years, people would discuss this awe-inspiring experience.

The following day, the Rebbe was so weak that he had to rest. All the chassidim were greatly pained by the Rebbe's state of health. In addition, no one knew what had affected the Rebbe so deeply to cause him such anguish. To their relief, he resumed accepting them into *yechidus* the following day.

A few days later, Reb Pinchas Reizes, who was extremely close to the Rebbe, asked him what happened.

---

88. During *Mincha*, *Veyichal Moshe* was read from the Torah and *Aneinu* was said in *Shemonah Esreh* as would be done on a fast day.

His face saddening for a moment, the Rebbe replied:

"When people enter into *yechidus,* they reveal the blemishes of their heart to me according to each one's particular situation. No matter what he tells me, my task is to find a reflection of that blemish on a more refined level in myself. Until I can correct it in myself, it is impossible to help him. Only through this inner work on myself can I guide and advise him in correcting it in himself.

"That day a person came to me and I was mortified by what he revealed to me that he had done. As hard as I tried, I could not find even a remote resemblance of that in myself.

"It dawned on me that perhaps the reason I could not relate to his issue is, G-d forbid, that it was deeply buried inside me. The idea that I could not acknowledge my own shortcoming made me tremble and brought me to return to Hashem from the depths of my heart."[89]

Sefer HaMaamarim Kuntreisim, pp. 712-3

---

89. Since the Rebbe could not find a counterpart to this person's problem in himself, he surmised that something terrible was hidden deep within him. This caused him terrible anguish and he did intense *teshuvah* to rectify the blemish.

The Source of
All Blessings

One of the main sources of income for the Jews of Russia was the tavern located in the inn. Each innkeeper sold his own or a friend's homemade vodka to the local population.

However, the prosperous times came to an abrupt end when the government forbade this practice. They decreed that every tavern had to buy its vodka from government-regulated brewers. This way the government was able to set high prices for the *mashke* and collect a tax on every bottle produced.

Woe to the person caught breaking the law. His entire stock would be confiscated and he would be forced to pay a heavy fine. This decree affected many directly, and, when the price of *mashke* became higher and higher, it affected almost everyone indirectly, for when people stopped visiting the taverns, many lost their livelihoods as a result. The financial situation became extremely dire.

After meeting to decide what could be done about the situation, the chassidim decided to send a small delegation to the Alter Rebbe and ask the Rebbe for a *brochah*. The delegation chosen consisted of HaRav DovBer, the Alter Rebbe's oldest son (and future successor); HaRav Aharon HaLevi, one of the Alter Rebbe's most outstanding students (known as the Starishela); and Reb Pinchas, his faithful chossid.

Hearing their heartfelt plea, the Alter Rebbe replied, "In order to receive the *hashpoah* from Above, one has to make a vessel." He then said, "And the proper vessels are love and brotherhood — not jealousy or tale-bearing. As we see in *Birchas Kohanim*, the *Kohanim* first lovingly bless the Jewish people — that there should be love and harmony among them — and only then do the *Yidden* receive the three benedictions that encompass all the general aspects of their lives."

Shortly afterwards, the Alter Rebbe entered the *beis midrash*, walked onto the *bimah* and said: "Hashem gives sustenance to all the living with kindness — and not only through a distillery.

"When one does a kindness to another by helping him find a livelihood, he is really just helping him find the *possibility* of a livelihood. But when Hashem shows kindness, that itself is the livelihood because Hashem's *brochah* for sustenance *guarantees* the sustenance. However, it is necessary for one to make a vessel to receive Hashem's kindness — and that is love and brotherhood."

When the Frierdiker Rebbe related this story in 5698 (1938), he concluded it by saying, "That year chassidim saw a *shefa* of livelihood in abundance."

He then said, "At this moment we are [also] in need of this *brochah* [for *parnossah*]. However, we need the [Alter] Rebbe to say it. But since the words of *tzaddikim* are eternal, it means their words are here; they are just concealed and have to be revealed."

The Rebbe repeated these words of his saintly father-in-law, the Frierdiker Rebbe, on Pesach 5718 (1958)[90] and said that since his words are eternal, it means they, too, are in effect now.

May there be true love and brotherhood amongst us, and may Hashem give all of us an abundance of parnossah; with all worries and anxiety about our livelihood removed from our midst. May this be a harbinger to the removal of all our worries with the coming of Moshiach Tzidkeinu *speedily in our days.*

---

90. Printed in *Toras Menachem*, vol. 22, p. 272.